How to Buy a Home When You Can't Afford It

Other McGraw-Hill Books by Robert Irwin

Buying a Home on the Internet

Home Buyer's Checklist

How to Get Started in Real Estate Investing

How to Find Hidden Real Estate Bargains

The McGraw-Hill Real Estate Handbook

Pocket Guide for Home Buyers

Robert Irwin's Power Tips for Buying a House for Less

Tips and Traps When Buying a Condo, Co-op, or Townhouse

Tips and Traps When Buying a Home

Tips and Traps for Making Money in Real Estate

Tips and Traps When Mortgage Hunting

Tips and Traps When Negotiating Real Estate

Tips and Traps When Renovating Your Home

Tips and Traps When Selling a Home

How to Buy a Home When You Can't Afford It

Robert Irwin

McGraw-Hill

New York   Chicago   San Francisco   Lisbon   London
Madrid   Mexico City   Milan   New Delhi   San Juan
Seoul   Singapore   Sydney   Toronto

Library of Congress Cataloging-in-Publication Data

Irwin, Robert.
    How to buy a home when you can't afford it / Robert Irwin.
        p.   cm.
    ISBN 0-07-138518-5 (alk. paper)
    1. House buying—United States. 2. Low-income housing—
United States. 3. Housing—Finance. I. Title.

HD1379.I6512 2002
643'.12'0973—dc21   2002006629

McGraw-Hill

A Division of The McGraw·Hill Companies

6 7 8 9 0 DOC/DOC 0 9 8 7 6 5 4

ISBN 0-07-138518-5

This publication is designed to provide accurate and authoritative information in regard to the subject matter covered. It is sold with the understanding that neither the author nor the publisher is engaged in rendering legal, accounting, futures/securities trading, or other professional service. If legal advice or other expert assistance is required, the services of a competent professional person should be sought.
                     —*From a Declaration of Principles jointly adopted by a Committee*
                            of the American Bar Association and a Committee of Publishers

McGraw-Hill books are available at special quantity discounts to use as premiums and sales promotions, or for use in corporate training programs. For more information, please write to the Director of Special Sales, Professional Publishing, McGraw-Hill, Two Penn Plaza, New York, NY 10121-2298. Or contact your local bookstore.

This book is printed on recycled, acid-free paper containing a minimum of 50% recycled, de-inked fiber.

CONTENTS

1. Homes Are More Affordable Than You Think   **1**

Pie in the Sky?   2

2. How Much Does a House Really Cost?   **3**

What's the Real Cost of Home Ownership?   3
PITI—The True Costs of Home Ownership   4
What Are My Tax Breaks?   5
Can Alternative Financing Reduce My Payment?   7
Can I Trade Points for Lower Payments?   8
What If I Have Little to No Cash?   10
What If I Have Credit Woes?   10
Where There's a Will There's a Way   11
Affordability Quiz   12

3. How Much Can You Really Afford to Pay?   **13**

How Big a Payment Can I Afford?   13
The Trouble with Pre-Approval   15
Where Do I Get Pre-Approved?   16
Budgeting Surprises   17
How Do I Come Up with Cash?   17
Can I Share a Purchase?   20

4. How to Afford a Home When Prices Seem Too High   23

Why Should I Identify the "Next Best" Neighborhood?   23
Farm the Neighborhoods   25
Look for the Smallest Lot, Worst House in the Area   26
Should I Make Lowball Offers?   29
Should I Consider a Turn-Around Area?   30
Attributes Turn-Around Neighborhoods Should Have   31
How Do I Look for Highly Motivated Sellers?   32
Should I Consider Foreclosed Properties?   34
What about Checking Out the Internet?   35
Home Affordability Quiz   36

5. The Condo, Co-op, and Prefab Alternatives   39

Is It a Different Lifestyle?   39
Are They Really Cheaper?   40
What's the Difference between a Condo and Co-op?   41
What Is a Townhouse?   42
How Do I Get a Good Deal When Buying a Condo or Co-op?   43
What Should I Be Wary of When Buying?   46
The Condo or Co-op Decision   50
What about Mobile Homes?   50
Condo, Co-op, and Prefab Alternatives Quiz   54

6. Buying from a FSBO Seller   57

What the Heck Is a FSBO?   57
How Do I Find a FSBO Seller Who'll "Give Me the Commission"?   58
How Do You Handle Paperwork in a FSBO Deal?   60
What about Arranging for Inspections and Getting Repairs Done?   60
How Do I Negotiate with the FSBO Seller?   61
What Do I Do Once We're Agreed?   63
Where Do I Find FSBO Sellers?   64
How Do I Introduce Myself to a FSBO Seller?   64
Should I Really Try Buying from a FSBO Seller?   65
Will an Agent Really Negotiate with a FSBO Seller?   66
FSBO Quiz   66

7. Cutting Costs with Fixer-Uppers   69

What's Involved in Buying a Fixer?   69
How Much Cash Is Involved?   70
What about the Timing?   72

How Do I Find a Fixer?   73
How Do I Evaluate a Fixer?   77
How Do I Know How Much to Offer for a Fixer?   81
Don't Overestimate What You Can Do   82
How Do I Get the Seller to Accept My Offer?   83
How Do I Structure the Deal?   85
Can I Really Do It?   86
Funds That You'll Need to Complete Your Fixer-Upper   86

8. Building Your Own Home   89

How Hard Is It?   89
Arrange for the Financing   91
Find and Buy a Lot   94
Get a Set of Building Plans   97
How Do I Hire a Contractor and Subs?   99
How Do I Do the Actual Work?   100
Finish the Financing   106
Building a Home Quiz   107

9. How to Afford a Home When You Have Credit Problems 109

Why Good Credit Is Important   109
How Does the Lender Know If You'll Repay?   110
Who Are the Lenders Who Evaluate Your Score?   111
Can Every Category Get Financing?   113
Can You Improve Your Credit Rating?   115
Can I Be Approved for a Mortgage If I Agree to Changes?   120
Can I Have Bad Credit Fixed?   120
What If I'm Having an Argument with a Creditor?   122
What Sorts of Explanations Will Lender's Accept?   123
What about Mistakes Made by the Credit Bureau?   124
How Do I Get a Copy of My Credit Report?   126
What If I Have No Credit?   126
Is It Hard to Establish Credit?   126
What Do I Do If I Need to Get a Mortgage Right Now and Don't
   Have Credit?   128
What about Getting Someone to Co-sign?   128
Credit Quiz   129

10. Finding a More Affordable Mortgage   131

Why Should I Consider an Adjustable-Rate Mortgage?   131
How Does an ARM Work?   132

The Basics of an ARM   134
What Is an Index?   134
What Is a Margin?   137
What Is an Adjustment Period?   138
What Are Steps?   139
What Are Interest-Rate Caps?   141
What Are Mortgage Payment Caps?   141
What Is Negative Amortization?   142
Should I Beware of Prepayment Penalties?   144
Caps Can Work against You   145
What If You Have Both a Monthly Payment Cap and an
    Interest-Rate Cap?   146
What Are the Types of Adjustable-Rate Mortgages?   146
What about a Convertible Option?   147
Affordable Mortgages Quiz   148

11. Affordable Mortgage Programs   **151**

Program Highlights   152
What Are the Fannie Mae and Freddie Mac Loans?   154
Where to Find Fannie Mae and Freddie Mac Loans   155

12. Affordable Housing Programs   **157**

What Is a First-Time Home Buyer?   157
How Do I Find Out about the Various Mortgage Programs?   158
Are There Any Special Fannie Mae Programs?   159
What about the FHA?   160
How Do FHA Mortgages Work?   160
Other Advantages of FHA Loans   163
Veteran Mortgages   165
Other Contacts   168
Affordable Housing Quiz   169

13. Find an Agent Who Will Work with You   **171**

Why Should I Care about Agent Loyalty?   171
How Do I Find a Loyal Agent?   172
Will All Agents Return Loyalty?   173
How Do I Interview an Agent?   175
Should You Work with a "Buyer's Agent"?   178
How Do I Determine Whom My Agents Represent?   179
Will a Buyer's Agent Represent Me Better?   180
Do I Really Have to Pay a Buyer's Agent?   181

Should I Sign a Buyer's Agent Agreement?   182

Should I Ever Work with More Than Just One Agent?   184

Should I Work with a Salesperson or a Broker?   184

Should I Work with an Independent Agent or One Who Represents a National Company?   185

Agent's Quiz   186

14. Negotiating with a Seller   189

Working with the Purchase Agreement?   189

How Much Time Should You Give the Seller to Accept Your Offer?   190

How Much Should You Offer Below the Asking Price?   191

What Terms Should Your Offer Contain?   192

What If the Seller Accepts Your Offer?   193

What If the Seller Rejects Your Offer?   193

What If the Seller Counters?   194

How Long Should You Counter When You're Not Close?   195

When Should You Send the Ultimatum?   195

Seller's Negotiation Quiz   196

15. 12 Steps to Buying an Affordable Home   199

Step One: Get Pre-Approved   199

Step Two: Find an Agent   199

Step Three: Find the Property   200

Step Four: Make an Offer—Negotiate   200

Step Five: Open Escrow   200

Step Six: Put Your Deposit in Escrow   201

Step Seven: Get Your Financing   202

Step Eight: Inspect the Property   203

Step Nine: Do a Final Walk-Through   204

Step Ten: Deposit Money into Escrow   205

Step Eleven: Sign the Papers   205

Step Twelve: Get the Key!   206

Steps to Closing Quiz   207

Appendix A. Amortization Table   209

Appendix B. Affordable Loan Programs   211

Index   221

1

Homes Are More Affordable Than You Think

There are 65 million homes in this country and in any year about 7 million, or 10 percent, are for sale. These run the gamut from brand-new houses to properties more than 100 years old. They include single-family homes, condos, and co-ops. Some have plenty of land; others are on postage stamp–sized lots. Some are single story; others as much as three stories tall. Some are in the city; others are in rural areas. And prices run the gamut from under $100,000 to well over $1 million.

All of which is to say there is no shortage of housing opportunities out there. If you really want to buy a home, there is certainly something available that you can afford no matter your financial condition. The real questions you need to ask yourself are:

- Do you really know how much house you can afford? (It could be much more than you think!)

- Do you know where to look? (In every locale there are hidden bargains.)

- Do you know how to get financing for all, or almost all, of the purchase price?

- Do you know how to come up with the cash that's needed?

- Do you know how to deal with bad credit (if that's your problem)?

- Do you know how to handle real estate agents and sellers so they will really help you buy?

If you think you can't afford to buy a home, chances are you're very wrong. While housing prices have soared in recent years, making huge profits for home owners, those who haven't yet bought don't have to remain on the outside looking in. You, too, can join the real estate boom. You, too, can buy a home.

Pie in the Sky?

Whenever I hear someone saying something's doable that I think is pretty much impossible, I'm inclined to question that person's credibility, if not sanity! When I say, "Yes, you can afford to buy a home," you may be thinking the same thing. You may be wondering if I'm simply building castles in the air. It's very easy to say it's possible to buy a home, but can I deliver?

Let me respond by saying that I've been in real estate for more than 3 decades and I've seen people in all sorts of financial condition buy homes. I've seen people in bankruptcy purchase property. I've seen people with absolutely no money and terrible credit buy homes. I've even seen people who are unemployed purchase a house.

No, they may not be buying mansions or riverfront lots, but they, nevertheless, are able to make a good home purchase. If you can legally enter into a contract you, too, should be able to buy a home. It's simply a matter of knowing how.

In this book, you'll see how you can buy a home even though you thought you couldn't afford one.

2

How Much Does a House Really Cost?

If you're renting, or haven't bought a home for some time, chances are that you'll get sticker shock when you begin to look at purchasing a house. Homes have gone up in price since the late 1990s and many areas have seen escalating costs in this century. All of which means that homes, both resale and new, are very costly.

However, that doesn't mean that homes are impossible to buy. Before you throw up your hands and decide that you simply can't afford a home, I suggest you do two things. First, discover how much it really costs to own a home. Second, take a very close look at your own income and budget to see what you really can afford.

What's the Real Cost of Home Ownership?

As we all know, there are two elements to buying a home: the down payment (plus closing expenses) and the monthly mortgage payment. The down, in decades past, used to be the big obstacle. But with more liberal loans available today, you often can get into a home with very little down payment. Indeed, if your credit is good and you purchase a property for around $300,000 or less, you can even get in for nothing at all down! (We'll go into great detail on how to lower the down payment as well as how to handle credit problems in later chapters—especially Chapters 9 through 12.)

Today, for most people the real problem is not the down, but the monthly payment, which becomes the real cost of home ownership, and is what we'll begin with in this chapter.

Real estate people like to refer to the monthly payment on a home as PITI. That stands for the **p**rincipal and **i**nterest on the home mortgage plus **t**axes and **i**nsurance, all of which are the basic costs.

TRAP

Of course, there are additional costs for maintenance and repair. Unfortunately, few agents emphasize these to buyers and, particularly if the home is older or in need of work, they can crop up as nasty surprises. Nevertheless, if you have a good home inspection, you should know in advance what immediate repairs are needed. And, if you do the home maintenance yourself, over time you can reduce much of the expense.

$$
\begin{array}{r}
\text{Principal} \\
+ \text{ Interest} \\
+ \text{ Taxes} \\
+ \text{ Insurance} \\
\hline
= \text{Monthly Payment}
\end{array}
$$

For now, we'll just consider the basic expenses as PITI.

PITI—The True Costs of Home Ownership

Let's split PITI into two groups—principal and interest and then later taxes and insurance. To begin, how much P and I can you afford?

Trying to figure this out is like trying to determine which came first, the chicken or the egg? You can't know how big the principal and interest payment will be until you know how high a mortgage you'll get. And you won't know how high a mortgage you'll be able to get until you determine how big a P and I you can afford!

Often the best way to determine your principal and interest payment is by simple trial and error. For example, see how much the monthly payment is for a $100,000 mortgage. Then try a $150,000 mortgage. Then a $200,000 mortgage. At each level you'll get a different monthly payment. If you'd like to buy a house in the $250,000 range, take a look at how big the P and I will be between $225,000 and $275,000. That will give you a strong clue as to affordability. But how do you calculate the P and I?

One way is to use Appendix A at the back of this book. Another way is to go online to one of the many mortgage sites (such as eloan.com, quicken.com, mortgage.com, and so on) and use the site's calculator. Just plug in the mortgage amount (say, $250,000), the current mortgage interest rate (which the site will tell you or which you can get by checking your local newspaper for fixed-rate 30-year loans) and the length of the loan (typically 30 years). Almost instantly you'll be shown the monthly payment.

Now play a little "what if" game. Change the amount of the loan and watch the monthly payment go up or down. Change the interest rate and see the same thing happen. Similarly, watch the monthly payment soar if you drop down from a 30-year to a 15-year loan.

This experiment will give you a sense of what it costs to borrow money at the time you are looking. Remember, the P and I are the biggest part of the monthly payment. But, there are also T and I, taxes and insurance.

Determining the cost of taxes and insurance requires some expert help. The easiest way to find out what the taxes and insurance are going to be on any property is to ask any good real estate agent. He or she should be able to give you a highly accurate estimate of what your monthly T and I costs will be on any property.

Now, just add all the figures together—P and I and T and I. This is your monthly payment. Wow, high, isn't it!

Is the PITI too high for you? You may be able to lower it! (A very rough rule of thumb is that you can afford about one-quarter to one-third of your income for PITI.)

The exercise you just did will give you a rough estimate of your raw monthly payment. However, in the real world chances are your true monthly cost will be far less. There are two reasons why:

1. You'll very likely get a tax break.
2. You'll have the option of getting alternative (lower cost) financing.

What Are My Tax Breaks?

First, there's the tax deduction you can take on mortgage interest payments. This will help offset your montly payment.

Most home owners, except those in the very top tax brackets, can deduct all of their mortgage interest (on up to a $1 million loan) and property taxes from their ordinary income. This means the amount of the monthly payment is deceptive. The actual cost is much less than the monthly check you write.

If you've been a home owner, you'll immediately know what I'm talking about. If this is news to you, however, consider the following:

Let's say that your PITI is $1,000 a month broken down as follows:

Principal	$ 35
Interest	835
Taxes	100
Insurance	30
Total	$1,000

Remember, you can usually *deduct* the interest and the taxes from your regular income. In our example, this comes to $935 month. That's a hefty deduction. If you're in the 28 percent tax bracket, for example, it means a cash savings *each month* of $262.

Thus, when you subtract the amount you'll save on taxes from the monthly payment, you suddenly discover that the true payment is much lower. In this case, instead of $1,000 a month, it's actually $738. You've saved almost a third. Now, that monthly payment should look far more attractive. Of course, the lower your tax bracket, the less the savings; the higher your bracket, the greater the savings.

TRAP

I've known neophyte real estate agents who have given buyers the wrong advice here. They've said you simply deduct your property taxes and interest from your income taxes. It's important to understand that you do *not* just subtract the interest and taxes from your tax liability. That would be a credit, which this is not. Instead, you deduct the interest and taxes from your total ordinary income and then recalculate your taxes. The wrong way would give you a 100 percent tax savings. The right way gives you a savings based on your marginal tax rate.

Of course, I'm sure some readers are saying that it's one thing to get a tax savings that comes at the end of the year and quite another to have to make a hefty house payment each month. However, if you're salaried and receive a monthly, weekly, or biweekly paycheck, you can elect to have the tax savings added back into your paycheck. Thus, in our example, your monthly earnings could be $262 higher. Yes, your payment on the house would remain at $1,000. But you'd get $262 more cash in your paycheck to help pay for it. Just instruct your employer to include additional deductions up to the allowable amount for your interest and property tax.

It goes without saying that your accountant or tax adviser should take a look at your income and your housing expenses and advise you on this important decision. Generally speaking, however, the tax savings of owning a property are one of the big incentives to buying. And it is one of the ways that your monthly house payment can be brought down.

Can Alternative Financing Reduce My Payment?

Another method of lowering your monthly payment is to juggle the financing. Often you can cut your monthly payment by as much as another third simply by getting a different type or style of mortgage.

While we'll go into mortgages in greater detail in Chapters 10 and 11, for now let's just consider some of the possibilities that are available.

When most people speak of real estate financing they are talking about a 30-year loan with a fixed interest rate in which the payments do not change over the life of the loan. This type of financing has been in place since the late 1930s and is still widely available today. However, it is not necessarily the least expensive.

TIP

All financing is based on an interest rate. Reduce the interest rate and the monthly payments go down.

If you go to any two lenders at any given time and look for a 30-year, fixed-rate loan with no points (we'll go into that next), chances are the interest, and hence the monthly payment, will be almost identical.

However, one lender may be willing to give you a much reduced interest rate *if* you are willing to accept an ARM (adjustable-rate mortgage).

ARMs can be loans with lower payments. They've been available since the 1970s and are loans in which the interest rate is tied to an index, such as the rate for Treasury bills. What this means is that over the course of the loan, if interest rates on that index go down, so too does the interest rate on your mortgage. And, consequently, so do your monthly payments (in most cases). If the index goes up, so do your monthly payments.

TIP

Adjustable-rate mortgages are tied to indices that are typically very sensitive to overall inflation and interest rates in the bond market and elsewhere.

The key point, however, is that in exchange for giving lenders flexibility, they will typically give you a lower initial interest rate, and consequently, lower initial monthly payments. This initial rate can be as much as a third or more lower than for a fixed-rate mortgage. Thus, if you were borrowing $200,000 and the fixed rate was 7 percent, the adjustable rate might be as low as 4 percent. The difference in monthly payments is between $1,331 and $955, a substantial savings!

Of course, there's a catch. The initial low rate doesn't usually last very long, sometimes only a year; sometimes only a month. That depends on what kind of an adjustable loan you're able to negotiate with your lender.

As noted earlier, we'll have more to say about this complicated subject in later chapters. But for now, just keep in mind that you can dramatically reduce your mortgage payment, at least initially, by negotiating a different kind of loan from a lender.

Can I Trade Points for Lower Payments?

Yet another method of reducing your monthly payments is to pay more cash up front (points) on your mortgage. Points are a one-time fee that lenders can charge when you obtain your mortgage. A point is equal to 1 percent of your loan. Thus, two points on a $200,000 mortgage are equal to $4,000 in cash.

If you've looked at mortgages at all, you'll quickly realize that lenders often quote them at such-and-such interest rate plus points. For example, the loan might be for 7 percent interest plus 1 point.

If you're in the position of having some extra cash (unfortunately, few of us are, but it does happen!), you can offer to pay more than 1 point in exchange for the lender lowering the interest rate. For example, you might offer to pay 4 points in exchange for a lower 6.5 percent loan. That will significantly lower your monthly payments on a $200,000, 30-year loan by about $100 every month.

TIP

Yield is all that lenders are concerned about. It is the total amount of return on their cash investment. For example, if one loan is at 6¾ percent at two points, another is at 6⅞ percent at one point, and yet another at 7 percent and no points, from a lender's perspective they all can yield 7 percent. They are all the same loan. Most points are interchangeable with the interest rate.

Thus, you can often negotiate with a lender to pay more points (cash) up front in order to reduce your interest rate and, consequently, your monthly payments. You might conceivably get your interest rate knocked down a half percent or more in this fashion. Alternatively, if you're a good negotiator, you may be able to get the seller to pay those points to get that interest rate knocked down! We'll have more to say about negotiating in Chapter 14.

TIP

Most points spent to obtain a mortgage when you're buying a home may be deductible in the year of purchase. That's another big consideration. Check with your accountant.

Of course, it works the other way as well. If you're cash poor, you may be willing to pay a higher interest rate (and a higher monthly payment) for no points, which means you need less cash up front.

What If I Have Little to No Cash?

As I've just suggested, these days it's possible to get into a home with little to nothing down. I can remember when couples would save for years in order to get $10,000 or $20,000 to put down on a home. They did it because they realized the value of home ownership. They also did it because the best financing available was a mortgage for 80 percent of the value of the property, meaning they typically had to come up with 20 percent down. (Houses, of course, were much lower priced in those days!)

Today, there are all sorts of mortgages out there designed expressly for people who are strapped for cash. You can get a mortgage for 90 percent of the value of the property, or only 10 percent down. If you're buying a $200,000 home that means you only need to come up with $20,000 in cash, plus closing costs of about $7,000 or $8,000.

Too much, you say? All right, you can get a mortgage for 95 percent of the value of the property, or 5 percent down. Now your down payment is only $10,000, plus closing costs.

Still too high, you say? Okay, what about a mortgage for 100 percent of the value with nothing down? Now you only need to come up with closing costs!

But you still complain about where you're going to get that $7,000 or $8,000?

How about a mortgage for 103 percent of the value, including closing costs and almost no cash! Now don't tell me you can't come up with a grand or so to buy a house!

All of these mortgage types are readily available, if you don't exceed the limit for "conforming" loans—currently $307,000. You'll need a strong income and very good credit. But given that, you can get this type of financing.

What If I Have Credit Woes?

I'm sure I've just touched a sensitive nerve with some readers by mentioning the word *credit*. Some of us are simply credit-challenged.

Often, because of no fault of our own (layoffs, illness, divorce, and so on), our credit is shot. We simply have terrible credit and, as such, cannot qualify for those wondrous loans just mentioned. We're out of luck, right?

No, not at all. Even if you have bad credit, you too can buy a house. There are special loans designed just for those who are credit-challenged. We'll discuss them in Chapters 9 and 11.

And if your credit is really terrible, you can always assume someone else's old existing loan. Or buy from a seller who is willing to handle the financing for you and doesn't really care all that much about your credit.

It's called "creative financing" and it's been around for decades. It's another alternative for those who have less than sterling credit or, for other reasons, want to structure financing outside the institutional mode. (I've seen some creative financing where the buyer didn't have any payments at all for a year or two!) Check into Chapter 9 for more on this.

Where There's a Will There's a Way

Our purpose in this chapter is not to define the different ways of buying a house that are open to you, but rather to broaden your horizon by suggesting opportunities. Few people who begin looking at homes actually realize the enormity of their options. Too many who could afford to buy a home pass up the chance because they simply don't realize that they can.

In the following chapters, we'll go into many different ways that you can afford to purchase a home given your current financial condition. However, I want to address one remaining issue that I'm sure some readers are rolling around in the backs of their minds. Am I saying that absolutely everyone can afford to buy a home?

Nope, not everyone. There's always bound to be someone who just can't do it.

What I am saying is that almost anyone in almost any financial situation can afford to buy a home if that person is willing to look into what's available and then make the effort to get out there and find the right property and the right financing.

AFFORDABILITY QUIZ

		YES	NO
1.	Are taxes and interest deductible?	[ ]	[ ]
2.	Can you take those deductions monthly?	[ ]	[ ]
3.	Can you get ARMs with low initial monthly payments?	[ ]	[ ]
4.	Can you trade cash for a lower interest rate?	[ ]	[ ]
5.	Can buyers get 103 percent financing?	[ ]	[ ]
6.	Can you get financing with challenged credit?	[ ]	[ ]
7.	Can you buy a home with terrible credit?	[ ]	[ ]
8.	Can buyers assume an existing mortgage?	[ ]	[ ]
9.	Can you get sellers to finance your purchase?	[ ]	[ ]
10.	Can you afford to buy a home?	[ ]	[ ]

ANSWERS

This is your easiest quiz. The answers are all yes! If you answered *no* to any of them, then you're not yet a believer. Continue reading. You'll see!

3

How Much Can You Really Afford to Pay?

Can you afford a $500 a month payment? What about $5,000 a month?

Can you put down $5,000? What about $50,000?

Do you know how much you really can afford?

I once had a partner in business who had the uncanny ability to keep all income and expenses in his head, almost down to the penny. So, if you were to ask him how we were doing at any given time, he could tell you to within a few dollars.

Perhaps you're the same way with your own personal income and expenses. On the other hand, if you're like most of us, you have an income (or perhaps two) and you spend money and hope that at the end of the month the one equals the other.

The fact is most of us simply don't have a clue as to just how big a monthly payment we really can afford. And we only have a hint as to how much money we can afford to put down. In this chapter, we're going to discover how to find accurate answers to both questions.

How Big a Payment Can I Afford?

At this point, some readers are surely expecting to find a budget listed that will help them determine their true expenses. These lists are indeed very helpful in demonstrating just how much you can afford. (You won't be disappointed. There's one coming up shortly!)

Other readers may be anticipating arcane formulas. Something like: You take your gross income, subtract all your long-term expenses, 50 percent of short-term expenses, apply this to your housing costs, and on and on. Actually, this is the way lenders still make "front-end" and "back-end" calculations on income versus expenses.

But here's a much simpler way of determining how much you can afford.

TRAP

It's actually financial profiling. The term *profiling* has gotten a lot of bad press in recent years, so lenders don't use it. However, keep in mind that *here* we're *not* talking about racial or ethnic profiling, but strictly financial. It's using profiles created from a database to come up with borrowers who are likely to succeed and those who are likely to fail and fall into foreclosure. This computer analysis can determine just how big a monthly payment you can afford to make and successfully pay back a mortgage.

If you've decided to buy a house and you want to learn just how much you can afford, go to a good lender or good mortgage broker (available under that heading in the yellow pages in every major city), or go online to one of the many Web lenders and get yourself "pre-approved."

Pre-approval is a process in which a lender takes a close look at your finances. The lender checks your income, especially your credit, and many of your expenses. You fill out a questionnaire consisting of about 60 questions. The lender sends the questionnaire along with the credit report (and your credit score, which we'll go into in Chapter 9) to an underwriter who feeds the information into a computer containing a database of more than 300,000 successful and unsuccessful borrowers. It spits out the maximum monthly payment you can afford. From that, you can deduce your maximum mortgage and, ultimately, your maximum price. Whatever it says, you can afford to take it to the bank—literally!

TIP

A few years ago, lenders used to give pre-approval letters that specified the loan amount a borrower could afford. However, these letters were often made invalid by rapid changes in the interest rate for loans. Today, many lenders only list a monthly payment that the borrower can afford. You have to work backward from the monthly payment using the current interest rate to find the maximum loan amount. And backward again from the maximum loan amount to the maximum purchase price.

Maximum monthly payment   = $1,000

@ 7 percent interest = $x,xxx Maximum mortgage

@ 95 percent LTV* = $x,xxx Maximum purchase price

*LTV stands for *loan to value*. It's the maximum the mortgage can be as a percent of the value of the property.

Usually, would-be buyers and borrowers are shocked by how much their pre-approval says they can afford. It's often much higher than the amount with which they may feel comfortable. Nonetheless, if the computer says you can, chances are excellent that you can! (However, budget lists, such as the one on page 18, are helpful in showing just where you can save money.)

The Trouble with Pre-Approval

While I'm touting pre-approval, it's important to understand that it's not without problems. It's important that you recognize this before you get pre-approved. Here are four common traps to avoid with pre-approval:

1. *Not to Be Confused with Pre-Qualified.* Years ago it was common practice for real estate agents to pre-qualify their borrowers. They would ask you a few rather personal financial questions and then, from your responses, determine how big a payment you could afford. From that, they could determine how big a house you could afford to purchase. Today, that almost never happens. Good agents will simply refer you to a lender or mortgage broker who will pre-approve you. When you come back with your pre-approval letter, both you and the agent know what you can afford. In truth,

there's less need for the agent to know your personal financial information than ever before. (Some financial information, such as your ability to come up with cash, will be essential for the agent to successfully negotiate for you.) Beware of the term *pre-qualified* as it signifies virtually nothing!

2. *Not to Be Done without a Credit Check.* Some mortgage brokers will simply get some information from you over the phone and then send you a pre-approval letter. This is *not* something you can take to any bank I know of. The minimum requirement for pre-approval is a credit check. This is often done automatically today as part of the *underwriting* process.

3. *Best Done by a Lender's Underwriter.* Underwriting is the process whereby secondary lenders, such as Fannie Mae or Freddie Mac (see Chapter 11), approve borrowers referred from primary lenders, such as your bank. Remember, the loan you get from your bank usually doesn't stay with your bank. It's sold on the secondary market. To be saleable, the borrower must have underwriter approval. A good lender will have your application approved by an underwriter. Today, this can be done electronically in a matter of minutes. After the underwriting process, the letter of pre-approval will state that the lender will commit to loan you funds based on a maximum monthly payment. This is the pre-approval that you can take to the bank.

4. *Best Not Issued by Mortgage Brokers.* What's your best source of mortgages? Mortgage brokers, which are individuals or companies who broker loans for lenders. They can get you the greatest variety and flexibility in financing. What's your best source of pre-approval? Mortgage brokers again, because they work with lenders. But beware. A pre-approval letter issued by a mortgage broker may not be worth the paper it's written on. The reason is that mortgage brokers do *not* fund loans themselves. They only broker them. You want your pre-approval commitment letter to come from a lender, the one who actually makes the loan.

Where Do I Get Pre-Approved?

Mortgage brokers are listed in the yellow pages. Lenders are banks, savings and loans, credit unions, mortgage bankers, and so on.

While these are all easy to find, you are probably best off with a recommendation from a friend who's successfully used one or a real estate agent you trust.

Online mortgage companies seem to come and go, particularly since the collapse of the Internet craze a couple of years back. Check a good search engine as well as some of the larger ones, such as quicken.com, lendingtree.com, or eloan.com.

Budgeting Surprises

I promised you a budget list and one follows. It can be filled out to help identify those areas where you can afford to cut and those where you will need to continue spending after you purchase a home.

The beauty of such lists is that they are really "what if" problems. Look at the list and see how you come out. Not enough there for that big monthly payment? Maybe there's something you can cut back on, such as some entertainment or recreation?

TRAP

Remember, what you put down on your list is to help make you feel more comfortable with the figure that a lender gives you as part of the pre-approval process. Your list is strictly for you. Don't make the mistake of thinking that it will carry any weight with a lender.

How Do I Come Up with Cash?

While determining from a budget how much money you have available to pay on a mortgage can be fairly complex, determining how much cash you have available usually appears to be much simpler. We just take a look at our bank savings account and there it is, like it or not.

In reality, however, you may have much more in the way of cash assets than you may have thought. On page 19 is a list of potential assets that you have that could be used to help purchase a home.

Most of us find a few pleasant surprises hidden in our assets once we start looking. A few of us find some really big surprises. For the

Budgeting to Determine How Big a Payment You Can Afford

Income

$_____ Net*

$_____ Increase after calculation for interest and property tax deductions

$_____ Increase after eliminating voluntary deductions

Less Expenses

$_____ Utilities (Gas, electric, water, garbage)

$_____ Phone

$_____ Cable/Satellite TV

$_____ Auto (Lease/Purchase pmt., ins., gas)

$_____ Food

$_____ Entertainment

$_____ Clothing

$_____ Child Care

$_____ Tuition (private schools)

$_____ Maintenance (gardening, painting, etc.)

$_____ Repairs

$_____ Child Support/Alimony

$_____ Medical (services, drugs)

$_____ Recreation (gym, sports, etc.)

$_____ Unpaid credit card debt**

$_____ Long-term loans

$_____ Total Expenses

$_____ Income Available for Mortgage Payment

*It's important to remember that your net monthly income is after voluntary deductions such as 401K contributions, which can be reduced or eliminated. Also remember, some of your involuntary deductions, such as for taxes, should be reduced because of the deduction you'll get for home mortgage interest and taxes, thus increasing your take-home pay. (See Chapter 2.)

**Unpaid credit card debt is the worst type of liability because it's paid back at extraordinarily high interest rates. Try to pay this down or refinance it into long-term debt before moving to make a home purchase. Lots of credit card debt may cause lenders to reject you for a mortgage.

Assets That Could Be Used to Help Purchase a Home

$_____ Cash from savings or checking account

$_____ Stock that could be sold*

$_____ Bonds that could be cashed in*

$_____ Life Insurance that could be cashed in*

$_____ Real estate mortgage owed to you

$_____ Other amounts owed you that you can call in

$_____ Sale of antiques of other valuables

$_____ Sale of car or boat (that you can live without)

$_____ Sale of other personal property

$_____ Borrowing from relatives (without immediate repayment)

$_____ Equity from other real estate that you own

$_____ Any other assets that you can convert

$_____ Total Assets

*Do not sell or cash in these assets without first consulting your accountant or financial adviser. You may need them for your overall financial health, retirement, or because of some other situation in your life.

remainder, a lot can be changed by an attitude makeover. For example, you might have $10,000 in a boat and trailer. Would you rather have a house? If you do, a sacrifice may be called for.

TIP

It may not be necessary for you to lose the cost of converting an asset to cash in order apply it toward the purchase of a home. Often converting to cash results in a loss in value. For example, you may have a piano worth $3,000. However, were you to sell it you might only realize $1,500 in cash. But you might offer it to a home seller as $3,000 worth of the down payment, and the seller might just accept. Thus, you wouldn't have lost the cost of cash conversion. But how realistic is it to expect a seller to accept assets instead of cash? You never know until you try. Remember, while the first rule in real estate is always *location, location, location!* the second rule is *everything is negotiable!*

Can I Share a Purchase?

There's one additional method of buying a property that has been tried now and again. It's sharing a purchase with another person (or couple). Here one person or party has the income, the other has the cash. They partner, sharing the purchase, with one being an investor, the other the occupant.

Equity or property sharing can be done between relatives, such as when parents provide the down payment and the child buys the home. Or between a home buyer and investor. Although it can be handled in a variety of ways, typically when the home is sold the party that put up the cash gets it back and then both parties split the hoped-for profits.

Sharing comes back into vogue every time there is a big jump in home prices as we've seen over the last few years. More people want to buy who have trouble affording a home and this suddenly looks like a good solution. And it can be.

A few words of caution, however. If you're thinking of using a sharing technique to facilitate a home purchase, be sure you get a contract in writing, even if it's with relatives. (Should I say especially with relatives!) People typically enter into partnership agreements with the best of intentions. However, over time one person's recollection can differ with that of another's. Hard feelings and worse can ensue when it all comes to a head and someone doesn't get what she feels entitled to. On the other hand, if it's all in writing, then it really doesn't matter what somebody remembered, or thought he remembered.

When putting a partnership sharing arrangement into writing, be sure that you spell out what happens in unexpected circumstances. For example, what happens if there's a loss instead of a profit? How is that shared?

Or what happens if one partner wants to pull out before the other? Or if one partner wants to keep the house and not sell?

It could cost several hundred dollars to get a good attorney to put it all down in writing. But it will be well worth it.

Equity or property sharing can be a great way to get the cash or come up with the income you need to purchase a house. Just be sure you handle it right so that there are no big problems later on.

There are many ways of increasing how much you can afford. We'll go into greater detail on these and other techniques in the next few chapters.

4

How to Afford a Home When Prices Seem Too High

There are few things that most people will agree upon. However, one exception is the high price of housing. Almost everywhere in the country, buyers complain about how much it costs to purchase a home. (Of course, sellers laugh all the way to the bank—and today's buyers will one day become sellers!)

None of this helps, however, when it's your turn to buy, particularly if you feel squeezed out of the market by high costs. What can you do when you really want to buy a home, but feel that prices are making home ownership unaffordable?

In this chapter, we'll consider some ways of getting around those prohibitively high values. No, this doesn't mean you're going to find your dream home in your dream neighborhood for 1940s prices. But it does mean that you just may be able to squeeze into a good house in a good area. Here are some tactics that may work for you.

Why Should I Identify the "Next Best" Neighborhood?

We've all heard that location is critical in real estate. It doesn't so much matter what you buy, as where you buy.

This is certainly true. But that doesn't mean you have to buy in the very best neighborhood. What it means is that there's a range of neighborhood quality. At the bottom are slums or places where you definitely would not want to live and where you shouldn't consider buying. (The one exception is in "turn-around" areas, which we'll consider shortly.)

At the top are the very best neighborhoods with the highest prices. You might want to purchase here, but the cost will be prohibitive. (Besides, some of these "top" areas suffer from a kind of exclusivity phobia that isolates them and actually makes them less desirable places to live.)

In between is everyplace else. While you may not be able to afford the *best* neighborhood, chances are you may be able to afford a *better* neighborhood. Prices are lower, yet these can be great places to live. What makes a *better* neighborhood? Here are five criteria to look out for. (Remember, these can be found in less than the *best* areas.)

Five Criteria for a Better Neighborhood

1. *Strong Sense of Neighborhood Pride.* You can see this in the way lawns and landscaping are kept up. The homes are freshly painted, broken-down cars are kept off the street and driveways, trash is quickly picked up by home owners, even if it's not theirs. These neighborhoods typically have a low incidence of rentals.

2. *Good Schools.* Studies have repeatedly shown that nothing makes a neighborhood stronger than strong schools. And nothing tears a neighborhood down faster than bad schools. Check out the school system by comparing local test scores against national and state averages. These are available at the local school district office. Some are also available online. While the scores may not be in the 90th percentile, anything above the 65th percentile should be considered a possibility.

3. *Low Crime Rate.* There's no such thing as "no crime rate." However, good areas tend to have a low incidence of "home" crimes, such as burglary and auto theft. The local police department can provide information not only by neighborhood, but often by block. Be wary of areas with a lot of graffiti. It suggests gang activity.

4. *No Detracting Development.* What you don't want is to buy a home next door to a toxic dump site or a factory or even a large shopping mall. (You want to be near shopping, not right on top of it with the accompanying traffic, lights at night, and noise). These

developments detract from a neighborhood. They may increase noise, pollution, and traffic. You definitely can buy into these areas cheaper. But you may have loads of trouble trying to resell later on.

5. *Easy Access.* It can be the best neighborhood in the world, but if there's no access to freeways, subways, trains, or buses, it has a big problem. Some of the country's best areas are isolated, which is great if you're retired or independently wealthy. But if you need to get to work every day, not having easy access can negate all the rest.

Farm the Neighborhoods

Once you know what to look for in neighborhoods, check out all those in the city or community in which you want to live. Look at them for pride of ownership, good schools, low crime, no bad features, and easy access. Try to pick several that you'd be pleased to live in. And then begin "farming" those areas.

Farming is a term used by real estate agents to identify a particular neighborhood or geographical area where they go back time and again to introduce themselves, drop off flyers, and answer neighbors questions all with the goal of someday getting listings. They plant "seeds of attention," which they hope will one day sprout into more business for themselves.

You should do the same thing. Initially, you may want to have an agent give you a tour of all the available properties in the area. All agents will be happy to do this in the hope that you'll buy through them (so they can collect a commission). We'll have much more to say about picking an agent in Chapter 13.

If you find a suitable home at an affordable price, buy it! However, if you don't, then start farming.

This means going back at least once a month, and preferably more often, down every street in the area you've selected. You're looking for signs of homes for sale. These include new listings, For Sale By Owner (covered in Chapter 6), people fixing up the property—perhaps in anticipation of selling—and so on.

Don't hesitate to stop your car and walk down the streets. If it's a weekend, talk to people who may be out watering their gardens or mowing their lawns. Spread the word you want to buy. You can't afford to pay a high price, but you're pre-approved and can move quickly. Leave your phone number.

TRAP

Don't simply rely on a real estate agent to cover this for you. If you don't buy initially, many agents will put you on a list of people to look for. But over time, this list gets dated and the agent may forget to look or may be busy with other clients. Farm the territory yourself if you really want to get a good buy.

Look for the Smallest Lot, Worst House in the Area

We all would like to live in a palatial estate with a dozen bedrooms and as many bathrooms. Having champagne taste on a beer budget is nothing new. However, be realistic. You just want to get into the neighborhood. Later you can sell what may be your first home and move up. But for now, getting in is the issue.

That may mean making sacrifices. In terms of location, it could mean getting a "flag" lot (see Figure 4-1), for example. This is a lot that has no frontage on the street—only a driveway. It is literally surrounded by other lots. Yes, it is less desirable, but it's less costly to purchase. (And, unfortunately, it will bring less when you resell.)

Consider a "key" lot (see Figure 4-2). This is the lot next to the house on the corner. The back of the corner lot faces this lot's side. Thus, this lot has the back of two properties facing it. Again, not as desirable and often less pricey.

Go for a smaller lot. Most people like room to roam. But today, with the cost of land often being higher than the cost of the home on it, getting less land can cut the price. Be careful to check for privacy issues, however. With less land you could end up looking out your window into your neighbor's living room or bedroom, which is not desirable at any price.

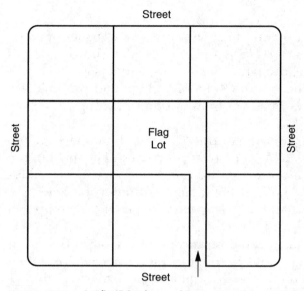

Figure 4-1. A "flag" lot has a driveway to the street but no frontage on the street.

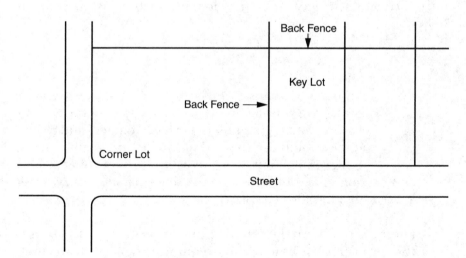

Figure 4-2. A "key" lot has the back of two properties abutting it.

TRAP

Don't think you can always cure privacy issues by erecting a fence or a tall stand of trees. Many housing tract's CC&Rs (Covenants, Conditions, and Restrictions) preclude fences above 4- to 6-feet high and prohibit "living fences" made of trees or other plantings.

Get the smallest house in the tract. Usually building developments have a variety of home styles and sizes. The bigger the home, typically, the more expensive. Find out what the smallest model is and keep an eye out for it. Yes, you might be cramped. But you could add on. And, in a few years, you could trade up to a bigger model.

Pay special attention to run-down properties. Homes that need paint and landscaping could be opportunities in disguise. Often there's a reason for their poor condition, particularly if they're located in an otherwise nice neighborhood. Maybe there's a divorce in progress. There might have been a death in the family. Someone could be out of work and the family is planning to leave the area quickly.

There can be a hundred motivations, all of which could mean an opportunity for you to obtain the home at a good price. Stop by and introduce yourself. Explain you're looking to buy. Ask if you can help out.

TIP

If you're hesitant to make these first moves on your own, have your agent do it. Agents, in general, are not bashful about going up to perfect strangers and asking if they would like to sell their home. Just keep in mind, however, that if you use an agent, there's going to be a commission involved. If the seller pays it, it may result in a higher sales price.

If a home is run-down, be sure that the problem is strictly cosmetic. Those problems lend themselves to quick, easy, and cheap cures. Try to determine if there's a more serious underlying problem, such as a bad roof needing replacement (costing upwards of $20,000); a cracked foundation needing fixing (costing as much as $15,000 to

$50,000 or more); or problems with the heating, plumbing, or electrical systems. Often the owners will be up front about these things.

If the home has a more serious problem, you may want to skip it, even if the price is lower. On the other hand, if you have a bent toward rehabbing, then by all means move forward. See more on this in Chapter 7.

Should I Make Lowball Offers?

What if you're looking in a neighborhood where homes cost about $275,000 and you know from having been pre-approved (see Chapter 3) that the most you can afford is $235,000? Do you simply move on and hope that a cheaper home will come up?

You can. Or you can lowball the seller. That means making an offer that's far below the asking price.

Will your offer be accepted?

Most times not. But occasionally, yes. It depends on how motivated the seller is to dispose of the home and how many other offers have recently been made on the property.

Remember, there is no one single price for homes in an area. Even identical homes go for a range of prices. When you check out neighborhoods, see what the lowest price was over the past year for any of the homes you are considering. This information should be readily available from any real estate agent connected with the MLS (Multiple Listing Service), which tracks such facts. Then aim for the lowest number, or perhaps even lower.

What you're doing is playing the odds. True, the odds favor a higher price in most cases. But every so often circumstances connect to produce a lower price. Make enough lowball offers and chances are one of them will get accepted! Also check into Chapter 14 on dealing with sellers.

TRAP

You may go through a lot of real estate agents if you persist in lowballing sellers. Agents like success. They like to get offers accepted. They'll encourage you to offer more. Or, if you can't, encourage you to accept lesser neighborhoods and homes. They'll insist that you be "realistic." However, your being realistic may only mean that it will become easier for them to get your offer accepted and to collect a commission. You don't want to make it easy for the agent; you want to get the best home you can afford. If that means wearing out the agent, who simply doesn't want to keep presenting lowball offers that aren't accepted, so be it. Remember that the agent is there to serve you, not the other way round.

Should I Consider a Turn-Around Area?

We discussed this briefly earlier. The conventional wisdom is to buy the most attractive home in the most desirable area you can afford. The reason behind this is that these are homes that will appreciate the most and the quickest. The last real estate boom of the late 1990s and the early part of this century confirmed this wisdom.

But things change. There are increasingly more people today who want to own homes, but who can't afford to buy the most expensive, not even close. Furthermore, many of those who did buy those pricey luxury homes a few years ago were taken down, financially speaking, by the collapse of the high-tech industry and the stock market. Where are all those high incomes to afford all those high-priced homes today?

All of which is to suggest that the next real estate boom may come not from the toniest area homes, but rather from modestly priced properties. Indeed, in many parts of the country, modest-priced homes are beginning to show steady price appreciation while their more expensive cousins languish unsold.

What does all this mean if you're struggling to afford any home? Just that some areas that might have been thought off-limits in the past may prove to be excellent opportunities today. I'm speaking specifically of turn-around neighborhoods.

Turn around is a euphemism for a former slum. Only it's a slum with attitude.

No one is suggesting that the best way for you to afford a house is to buy in a slum area. However, many slum areas today are seeing a resurgence of vitality. People that can't afford high-priced housing are turning to these low-priced, often run-down homes and are fixing up both the property and the neighborhood.

You can see this in the slum areas of many cities across the country. While some houses continue to look run-down, many in the neighborhood have been refurbished. They have new lawns, new paint, and a new attitude. And the owners have banded together into strong home owner associations to help control crime and gangs.

No, this type of housing is not for everyone. It is a challenge. But it's often the cheapest housing you'll find. And it may also have the greatest potential.

TIP

Check with the redevelopment council or board of your city to see if they have information on turn-around areas. Often, special low-interest, low-down financing is available as well as help with fixing up properties. There are also many national programs available. Check into www.fanniemae.com.

Attributes Turn-Around Neighborhoods Should Have

When evaluating a potential turn-around neighborhood, I always look for at least three attributes that it should have.

1. *Work in Progress.*   You never want to be the first on your block to try to turn things around. Rather, look for blocks where at least a quarter of the homes have already been refurbished and there's a strong home owner association present.

2. *Local Attraction.*   There has to be some reason for people to want this area. Is it close to downtown (a big plus these days when traveling congested roads can be a real turnoff)? Is it near a park or new commercial or office center (a sure supply of well-paid workers)? Is there some new development coming soon (check with local planning commissions to find out)?

3. *Not Crime Central.* While slum neighborhoods typically have higher crime rates than most suburbs, some are literally infested with crime. They are notorious for it. It may be organized in the form of gangs or the mob, or it may simply be the location where all the drug deals or murders occur. Check with local police authorities. They will quickly advise you. And stay away. Unless and until there are public works projects to reclaim these areas, they won't improve. In almost all cases, it's far too hard for individual citizens, even in groups, to overcome this.

TIP

Your biggest bargains can be found in turn-around areas. In parts of the city of Los Angeles, for example, home prices have shot up and the quality of life has dramatically improved in only a few short years as home owners reclaim older, run-down neighborhoods. Where a home might cost $350,000 in an outlying suburb, you might pay only half to a third that much in a close-in, run-down area. However, once perceptions about it turn around, the prices go right back up.

How Do I Look for Highly Motivated Sellers?

Not all sellers want to sell equally as bad. Some are just out there fishing. If they get a bite, they'll reel it in and take a look at how big it is. If it's not big enough, they'll throw it back.

Other sellers, however, are desperate to sell. They need to get out of their homes now. They will consider any reasonable (and some unreasonable!) offers. In the trade these are referred to as highly motivated sellers.

Now if you're a buyer, which type of seller would you like to deal with?

The highly motivated seller is the one who is most likely to accept your lowball offer. This seller is the one who offers you the best chance of getting into a house that you can afford.

But you may reasonably be asking what makes a seller highly motivated? There are typically five reasons.

Why a Seller Would Be Highly Motivated

1. The seller has bought another home and has to quickly sell this one in order to close the deal on the new home.
2. There is a job change to a different area necessitating a rapid move.
3. The seller has lost his or her job or for other reasons is in financial difficulty and needs to get out quick.
4. The seller has some other problem, such as a divorce, and simply must get rid of the house immediately.
5. For one reason or another, the seller can't make the payments on the property and must sell soon or lose it.

The next logical question is how do you determine the motivation of a seller. It's one thing to know what to look for, but quite another to find someone with that motivation.

The answer is that you ask. Ask the agent first. Very often highly motivated sellers will have told their agent that they must sell fast. This is the kind of information that the seller's agent will pass on to a buyer's agent, who will pass it on to you. You may be told, "Consider this home. The sellers want action today. They'll consider any offer." That's your call to action.

TIP

Another way of looking at motivation is speed. Any seller who must sell fast, for whatever reason, should be considered highly motivated. A seller who has plenty of time has no motivation to accept a lowball offer.

Consider asking the sellers. In your hunt for houses, you'll tour many properties where the sellers are present. Simply ask them why they're selling.

Expect to receive many varied answers. They might say, "We're just testing the waters. If we get a good offer, we'll move to a better home. Otherwise, we're happy here."

Forget this seller. Unless you offer full price, or close to it, you'll get no deal.

On the other hand, the sellers may say, "We've got to be in Phoenix so the kids can start school in three weeks. We're desperate!" Make the offer.

Ask neighbors. When you tour homes and the sellers aren't there, don't just go in and out of the house in question. Walk around the neighborhood a bit. If someone is outside working on her yard, strike up a conversation. Be forthright. Explain you're looking to buy a house, but are hard-pressed to pay full price. Does she know if this seller or any others in the area are very anxious to sell?

Neighbors know all sorts of things you'd never guess, frequently including the sellers' motivation. You might find a live one here.

Should I Consider Foreclosed Properties?

If you're willing to accept a certain amount of aggravation in your home search, you might want to consider looking at properties taken back by lenders. These can offer significant price reductions, allowing you to get into a neighborhood you might not otherwise be able to afford.

There are basically two types of foreclosures (as defined by their step in the process). The first is the traditional foreclosed property, where a lender is calling in the home loan because a borrower typically hasn't made the mortgage payments. You can buy this home from the borrower or seller directly, provided the foreclosure hasn't progressed too far. Or, you can buy it at a public auction if it has. This is very tricky, and I advise against it unless you've got someone very experienced to work with you.

The second type is called an REO (Real Estate Owned). These are properties the bank has taken back. It is now the owner, or seller, and is offering them directly to the public. The opportunity for a huge saving is not as great here. On the other hand, the inherent risks are also smaller.

Buying foreclosed property is generally considered the domain of real estate investors. However, there's nothing to prevent a first-timer from going right in and getting a terrific deal. Be aware, however, that it does involve learning more about the business, having your cash ready to go, and learning to live with a higher level of stress. If this sounds appealing to you, check with local agents and banks for properties they have available. Also, you may want to look into my book on real estate investing, *Buy, Rent, and Sell* (McGraw-Hill, 2001).

What about Checking Out the Internet?

Finally, don't limit your house-hunting search to physical properties. Check out virtual listings on the Internet.

It has been estimated that 95 percent of all homes for sale are also listed somewhere on the Internet. Almost all houses listed by Realtors® are also placed on the Web sites *www.realtor.com* or *www.cyberhomes.com.*

In addition, there are many other Web sites that cater to homes that are not listed, the so-called FSBOs (For Sale By Owner). Since these sites come and go, rather than list them here, I suggest you use a good search engine such as Yahoo or Lycos to find them. Then see what's available. You may find a very affordable bargain.

TRAP

Always consider homes listed on the Internet as potential purchases. If they seem like a good deal, call the agent or owner and then check them out just as you would a physical home. Don't even consider buying a home off the Internet without first seeing and going through the rigorous examination that you would use for any home you physically visited.

There are all sorts of ways to get around the high price of homes. Just keep in mind, however, that they all involve some active work on your part.

HOME AFFORDABILITY QUIZ

	YES	NO
1. Should I always look for the best neighborhood?	[ ]	[ ]
2. Is school quality an important neighborhood asset?	[ ]	[ ]
3. Should I stay away from high-crime areas?	[ ]	[ ]
4. Can I identify pride of ownership?	[ ]	[ ]
5. Should I consider neighborhoods with limited access?	[ ]	[ ]
6. Is a house near a toxic site a good buy because it's cheap?	[ ]	[ ]
7. Should I become a "farmer" when searching for homes?	[ ]	[ ]
8. Is a flag lot or a key lot out of the question?	[ ]	[ ]
9. Will I usually lose the deal on lowball offers?	[ ]	[ ]
10. Should I stay away from turn-around areas?	[ ]	[ ]
11. Does "work in progress" help a slum?	[ ]	[ ]
12. Should I ask a seller if he or she is motivated?	[ ]	[ ]
13. Can I ask a neighbor or an agent?	[ ]	[ ]
14. Should I pass on highly motivated sellers?	[ ]	[ ]
15. Are REOs a real option?	[ ]	[ ]

ANSWERS

1. No	9. Yes
2. Yes	10. No
3. Yes	11. Yes
4. Yes	12. Yes
5. No	13. Yes
6. No	14. No
7. Yes	15. Yes
8. No	

SCORING

12–15 You'll be in your own home soon!

 8–11 You need to broaden your options.

 5–7   Perhaps a reread of the chapter will help.

 0–4   You'll make a great tenant!

5

The Condo, Co-op, and Prefab Alternatives

As soon as you discover that affordability is an issue, you are sure to begin looking at housing alternatives and the first that will turn up are condominiums and co-operatives. If these don't pan out, you may even begin considering prefab or mobile homes or, as they are sometimes called, trailer parks.

There's nothing wrong with any of these alternatives. Indeed, one or another may prove just right for you. In this chapter, we'll go over just what each involves.

Is It a Different Lifestyle?

There's a tendency to think of a condominium or a co-op as simply a less expensive form of house. That's not the case. (Indeed, in some recreational or urban areas the condo or co-op may be as expensive as, if not more than, single-family homes!)

Actually, these types of living involve a modified lifestyle from that of a single-family home. Here are some of the similarities and differences.

Similarities to Single-Family Homes

- You have ownership.
- You pay taxes.
- You can sell or rent (subject to certain restrictions).
- You are the master of what you own, on the inside.

Differences from Single-Family Homes

- You own many areas in common with other owners.

- You pay monthly fees in addition to regular home costs.

- Neighbors are usually closer and you have less privacy.

- You may have amenities such as pools, tennis courts, and/or a clubhouse.

With a condo or co-op, what you actually get is shared ownership. There are often many recreational activities that go on and there's a board or HOA (Home Owners Association). These set rules that may include where you can park your car, how late you can have a party, and what type, if any, holiday decorations you can put up. You can participate as much or as little as you like, but be aware that the common rules will certainly affect you.

TRAP

There's a tendency to overlook the real differences between condos or co-ops and single-family homes and focus instead simply on the price. That's a mistake. Be sure you know what you're getting into before you buy. As I said, it's not just a cheaper form of housing. It's a different kind of housing.

TIP

Try it before you leap. If you're really not familiar with a condo or co-op situation, why not take six months and rent one? It will make you a believer one way or the other. And you won't have to make the commitment that purchasing involves.

Are They Really Cheaper?

Generally speaking, yes. While the percentage difference between a shared-lifestyle home and a single-family home will vary area to area, development to development, you can often pay as little as half the cost for the condo or co-op. In most cases, though, it will be more like 60 to 70 percent for roughly the same square footage.

Keep in mind, however, that cheaper going in means cheaper coming out. You'll probably get less for your unit when you sell than if you had purchased a single-family home.

TRAP

Historically, condos and co-ops have been the last to see price appreciation in boom periods and the first to go down in value when a recession hits. It's something to consider.

What's the Difference between a Condo and Co-op?

They're similar, yet as different as night and day. With a condominium you actually own real estate. You get a "fee simple" title, the highest form of land ownership.

Yet, if your unit is in a tall building, you may only own a theoretical airspace. For example, if you're on the third floor of a five-story condo complex, there are other owners on all sides of you sharing walls as well as above and below you, sharing ceilings and floors!

TRAP

Noise is a big concern with condos and co-ops. This is particularly the case with *conversions*, which are apartment buildings that have been converted to condos or co-ops. In new construction, the developer usually builds in noise barriers between units. In older apartment buildings, this often was not the case and it may not have been added during the conversion because of the extreme cost. Always try to check out a condo by coming in the evening when the neighbors are home and seeing if you hear their conversation, TV sets, stereos, and so forth through the walls. Once you own the place, you may be stuck with the noise.

The governing board of a condo complex is called the HOA (Home Owners Association) and is composed of members elected from the association members. Its job is to enforce the CC&Rs and bylaws that come with ownership, create rules to maintain the common areas of the development, and collect fees to pay for all of this. The HOA has extraordinary powers to control what you can do outside your unit since this is basically property held in common. What you do inside your unit is basically up to you, as long as it doesn't impinge on other owners (such as plugging up the plumbing or shorting out the electrical system).

Condominium developments are found in almost all states.

A co-op is more like a partnership. The co-op actually owns the real estate and you're given stock in the co-op as evidence of your ownership of your own unit. As with a condo, you may have other owners on all sides of you.

The governing body of the co-op is the Board of Directors, which is elected from the stockholders. It has all the powers of an HOA and more. Because the co-op tends to be a more closely knit organization, the co-op may have the power to determine how many people can live in your unit. If you sell or rent, it may have the power to veto or approve your choice of buyer or tenant based on their financial condition.

Co-ops are also found in most states, but sparsely. They are mostly congregated on the East Coast.

TRAP

Theoretically, co-ops can only approve or disapprove your buyers or tenants for financial reasons. However, stories abound of co-ops discriminating on the basis of the number of children in the family, medical history, ethnic background, race, and so on. Hopefully, this is not something you'll run into.

What Is a Townhouse?

I have heard people say, "I'm not buying a condo or co-op, I'm buying a townhouse!"

Wrong! There is no separate legal entity called a townhouse. Rather, you get either a condo or a co-op. What makes a townhouse distinctive is its shape. In a townhouse, there is no one else beneath you and no one else above you. There may, however, be units on all sides of you. In other words, you own down to the land below and the sky above. Your ownership as noted, however, is still in the form of either a condo or co-op, with all that entails.

Sometimes townhouses are referred to as PUDs (Planned Unit Developments). They are still condos with a townhouse orientation.

How Do I Get a Good Deal When Buying a Condo or Co-op?

As with single-family homes, there are many factors that influence price. Some are the same. However, some are quite different and are important to consider.

What to Consider before Purchasing

Location. This remains number one. However, now you're concerned not only with the overall location of the development, but with the location of the unit itself within the development.

As with single-family homes, you want to buy into a property that has the best possible location. This includes all of the following:

- Good schools
- Low crime area
- Close to a good residential anchor, such as near a beach or lake, downtown, or a desirable suburban location.
- A good mix of housing (single family as well as shared ownership).
- Easy access to freeways, mass transit, and airports so you can quickly get to a variety of employment opportunities.
- Close to shopping and recreation.

You want to avoid a development that is situated in "apartment city." In other words, the whole area is nothing but shared-unit developments and apartment buildings. This means a much increased density over single-family homes, which is a serious detracting feature to any future buyer.

Pay attention to how the overall development looks. A good-looking shared-ownership development will have an appealing front. The appearance should say that this is a respectable area where people are safe and free to have quiet enjoyment of their home. In other words, a place you would want to live. A guarded gate or a doorman helps both with appearance and security, but remember the cost of this will be coming out of your pocket.

Also pay attention to where the unit you're considering buying is located within the development. It's important to remember that not all locations within a development are equally valued. For example, you don't want to buy the unit that's located next to the garbage dumpster. You may pay less going in, but you'll have a really tough time reselling.

Here are some location features that are important:

1. *View.* When buying into a development that has a special feature, such as a view, be sure your unit has access to that feature. Otherwise, you'll be paying extra and not receiving the benefit. Also, does the unit face a tree-lined green belt or does it have a view of the driveway? While people like looking at trees, most of us don't have much fondness for watching asphalt. Beware of inside units. In some larger developments, the inside units simply face other units over a small courtyard. While it's true the inside units typically will cost less to buy, it's also true that it's hard to find a buyer for them at a reasonable price when it comes time for you to resell.

2. *Density.* This refers to how many people actually live within the development (and around it). Lower density is always more desirable. The fewer owners crowded together in an area, the more each of them will enjoy the property. There will be less noise, you will find it less crowded when you use the amenities such as the swimming pool or tennis court, and you'll find that you see your neighbors less often, which is something most people appreciate. Townhouses typically have the lowest density and, hence, are considered more desirable.

3. *Noise.* We've already touched on this. You don't want a noisy unit. To avoid getting one, be sure the unit you're considering:

- Isn't near a swimming pool.
- Doesn't face any busy street.
- Doesn't face a shopping center, school, or other facility where lots of people are around.
- Isn't near garages or carports where cars are constantly coming and going.

4. *Safety.* In some developments, some units are less safe because they're outside the perimeter fence or face the public street directly or even are close to the entrance. In a tall building, the ground floor units may be less attractive because they are easier to break into.

All of the above features may cause a unit to be priced less than a similar "safe" unit. Again, this is a case where it doesn't pay to be penny-wise and pound-foolish. Whenever there's a safety concern, try to avoid purchasing the unit. It will be less desirable and more difficult to resell later on.

As noted, a gate or guarded entrance helps with security. People will pay more for these (generally at least 5 percent more than a competing ungated or unguarded development) and they are usually easier to resell.

Layout. When you build units next to each other, there are inherent problems in the layout, or how the rooms flow into one another. Remember, in most units there are other units on at least two sides and sometimes top and bottom. This necessitates having windows only at the end and having a design that's long and narrow. The result is often a condo or co-op that is dark and not well lighted.

Creative room flow and lots of artificial lighting can overcome this to a great degree, however. Skylights, where possible, are also a great help.

TRAP

Pay special attention to the lighting when you first walk in. Is the place dark and narrow, reminiscent of a dungeon? Many condo and co-op units have this feel about them. You won't like living in a place like that no matter how affordable it may be.

Size. Although single-family houses come in all sizes, a typical house will be somewhere between 1,500 and 2,000 square feet.

On the other hand, although condos and co-ops come in all sizes, a typical unit will be somewhere between 800 and 1,200 square feet. In other words, they tend to be smaller.

TRAP

When you first begin looking at condos and co-ops, you'll sense that they are smaller than single-family homes. But after looking at them for awhile, you'll adjust to the lesser size and it will seem natural. Beware of this adjustment. You may be paying less simply because you're getting less. For example, if a 2,000-square-foot house sells for $200,000 and a 1,200-square-foot condo sells for $120,000, you're still paying $100 per square foot. At that price, however, the house is probably a steal and the condo or co-op is overvalued. A typical condo or co-op should cost less per square foot.

What Should I Be Wary of When Buying?

Again, the same rules apply as when buying a single-family home. However, there are a few additional concerns to worry about.

Rental Ratio. When looking for affordability, you're sure to occasionally run into a development where units are cheaper per square foot than others nearby, yet where everything else noted above seems okay. When that happens, ask your agent, the HOA, or Board what the ratio is between owners and renters.

Nothing sinks a condo or co-op development faster than to have a large population of tenants. This is not to say anything against tenants or owners who become landlords. Often large tenant populations occur when owners find they can't sell and rent out their units instead.

Tenants, not having the financial stake of owners, sometimes aren't as careful about noise, the number of people living in a unit, parties, and so on. Thus, with large rental popuiations, the lifestyle value of the complex tends to deteriorate.

TRAP

When the tenant-to-owner ratio reaches 25 percent, many lenders will stop offering mortgages. The lenders understand the problems that can occur when too many units are not owner-occupied.

The general rule is simple. The more tenants, the less desirable the development. Usually when the price is lower, there's a reason.

Lawsuits. We live in a litigious society. People sue people all the time and often over seemingly trivial concerns. You'll never see better examples of this than in shared-living situations.

Owners often sue the HOA or Board over strict enforcement of rules. The HOA or Board often sues owners for lack of compliance with the rules. There are often lawsuits against the original builder or developer for problems with construction. And on and on.

The problem is that in a shared-living situation, when there's a lawsuit against the development it's a lawsuit against you. Even if you win, there could be attorney and court costs. If you lose, there could be severe monetary penalties.

Thus, check out any condo or co-op development you are considering for both current lawsuits as well as their history of lawsuits. The more litigious the development, the greater the chances for financial loss and the better off you'd be skipping it.

TRAP

You may not be able to buy into (or later resell) a development with lawsuits. Lenders may freeze making any new mortgage loans when lawsuits are pending. The reason, quite simply, is that any future monetary awards might conceivably be payable before the mortgage, resulting in a potential loss to the lender.

You should demand a written statement disclosing all lawsuits involving the development from the seller and the HOA or Board. In most states, they are required to give this to you.

Reserves. Everything wears out over time. That includes roofs, water heaters, paint, and so on. When it's a single-family house, it's usually up to you to decide when to do maintenance and repair, and to come up with the money to cover it. With a condo or co-op, it's up to the HOA or Board to decide when, and then they have to pay for it.

Of course, they can't pay for it unless they have the money collected from you and the other owners. That's why in badly run developments there are often sudden and large assessments to cover such work.

In well-run developments, however, a certain portion of each month's fees is put into reserve. There they remain gathering interest until such time as they are needed to cover the painting, roofing, or whatever needs doing. No high special assessments are needed. (In some developments, you and not the HOA are responsible for roof repairs/replacement—check it out!)

TIP

In many states today, the law requires developments to maintain adequate reserves. Failure to do so can result in fines.

Be sure you investigate the reserves of the development you are considering. An accounting of the funds should be made available to you by the HOA or Board. The reserves should be reasonable. For example, money set aside for a new roof every 20 to 25 years, new central water heaters every 10 years, and so on should provide sufficient funds to cover the costs. If you're not sure, take this information to your accountant for an analysis.

Insurance.   The development needs liability insurance. I wouldn't consider anything less than $5 million, and $15 million would not be unreasonable.

The insurance is to cover the owners (you) in the event of a loss from an accident, a lawsuit, or some other calamity. Without insurance, you could be subject to a lien against your property for some untoward event.

Spikes in Fees.   Be sure you take a look at the history of fees for the development. Have there been times when there were sudden spikes, when fees suddenly went up 50 percent or even doubled?

This suggests bad management on the part of the HOA or Board. Spikes can be caused by sudden assessments to cover repairs, or to cover lawsuit losses, or anything else that the governing body should have anticipated, but didn't.

Also, sometimes when developments are first created, the fees are set unrealistically low. This helps to entice people to buy in. Then, after a few years, everyone wakes up and realizes the development needs much more money and fees jump through the roof.

Historical spikes in fees are a bad sign. What happened before could happen again.

TRAP

Beware of high monthly fees. Remember, you must pay these on top of your usual PITI (principal, interest, taxes, and insurance). They may significantly reduce the affordability of the development. In today's market, fees of under $200 monthly are considered fairly low. Fees ranging from $200 to $400 are considered moderate. And $400 and above are high.

TIP

Ask if the monthly fees include anything that you'd otherwise pay, such as fire, earthquake, flood, and hurricane insurance; and water, gas, garbage, and so on. If the fees cover some insurance and utilities costs, they may not be as high as they seem at first glance.

Onerous Rules. This final concern can be the most important to you. Remember, the single biggest difference between a shared-lifestyle and owning a single-family home is that you have to live under a set of rules.

Find out what the rules are. These can be obtained from the seller, the Board, or the HOA. Then read them very carefully. See if there are any that you simply can't abide by.

TRAP

Don't be under the mistaken belief that you will be able to change the rules once you're an owner. The hardest thing to change in a condo or co-op environment is the rules. It often takes an almost impossible to get two-thirds vote of all owners. In other cases, it takes a vote by the Board, which may have instituted the rule in the first place. Figure the rules are there to stay. It's up to you to decide whether you can or can't live under them.

Most of the rules will pertain to the design of the development. For example, they may say that no unit can be smaller than 1,200 square feet or larger than 1,500 square feet. Or that the HOA or Board must maintain all of the common areas. These are rules that few people will have any problems with.

Some, however, can be problematic. There may be rules that each owner is limited to parking one or two autos in the development. What are you to do if you have three?

There might be a rule prohibiting motorcycles. Or restricting the use of swimming pools by small children. Or limiting partying after 10 p.m.

You might argue, justifiably, that some or even all of the rules are not enforceable under the laws of your state. But what are you going to do? Bring suit against the HOA or Board (all the other owners) to force a change? Better to simply not buy in the first place!

The Condo or Co-op Decision

When affordability is the biggest issue, condos and co-ops will loom big as alternatives. However, from what we've seen here, it's important to remember that they are not simply less expensive single-family homes. They are a shared-lifestyle type of ownership, with inherent advantages and problems. Know what you're getting into before you leap!

For more information check out my book *Tips and Traps When Buying a Condo or Co-op* (McGraw-Hill, 2000).

What about Mobile Homes?

Mobile homes may be the most affordable housing anywhere. In an area where homes can cost $350,000, a nearby mobile home park may offer units selling for under $100,000—often far under. If affordability is an issue for you, you definitely should at least consider this alternative.

However, be forewarned that there's significant bias against mobile-home parks largely because of the image taken from the old trailer parks, some of which still exist. The image is of a trailer parked on a tiny lot, left to decay, perhaps surrounded by worn out appliances, cars, and so forth. It's an image of a slum.

That, however, does not in any way describe a modern mobile-home park. Yes, the units are mobile, prefabricated, and trucked to the location. But they are often surrounded by gardens with orderly streets and sidewalks. Often the parks have pools, spas, clubhouses, or even putting greens. In short, they are luxurious places to live.

What Is a Mobile Home?

There's a lot of confusion regarding mobile homes, or trailers, so let's just be sure that we're all talking about the same thing. What I mean are prefabricated homes that are trucked to a rental site and then placed there. The owners typically have a loan on the structure and pay rent to the site owner.

Some questions immediately arise here. First in importance, are these truly real estate?

The answer: no and yes. Depending on the state, the homes may be qualified as vehicles for which there is a licensing fee; or real estate, for which there are real property taxes to pay. Often the difference is determined by something as esoteric as how quickly wheels can be put on and the home can be made mobile again (some states have a 24-hour rule!).

TIP

Most owners keep their homes at least theoretically mobile since they prefer the usually lower vehicle tax than the much higher property tax. This means wheels and axles ready to be assembled and a foundation that can quickly be knocked out.

Mobile homes may be the best-kept secret in affordable housing. The only real problem that I've found with them is that there are so few mobile parks available.

TRAP

Most communities do not like mobile-home parks. The owners often do not pay local taxes, yet demand local services such as schools, fire protection, police, and so forth. (In a compromise in many communities, owners pay a fee and contract these services.) Hence, in many areas it has become almost impossible to get the necessary permits to build new mobile-home parks. This means that often the only ones available are decades old.

How Do I Find Out about Mobile Homes?

There are really only two ways. Check a search engine on the Web for builders. They can refer you to local dealers and these dealers know where parks are available. Some of the bigger builders are:

www.skylinecorp.com

www.fleetwood.com

www.championhomes.com

On the other hand, if you already have a community in mind, then check the yellow pages for mobile-home parks. If there are any in the area, go visit them. There are almost always existing units for sale. You may be able to pick up a suitable one in a good area for $50,000 to $75,000!

What Should I Watch Out For?

It's sort of like buying a combination house and car. You need to use the sort of diligence in inspection that you would use for both. You also need to be aware of the rent charged by the park and the likelihood of it going up significantly.

Condition. Just as you would have a stick-built home professionally inspected, have a mobile home checked out. You want to be sure it's structurally sound, the appliances all work, the roof is in good shape, and so on.

Also, have the seller provide a termite clearance. This is probably going to be a necessity before any lender will offer financing.

Rental Rate. Remember, in most cases you won't own the land under the trailer. You'll be renting it.

Find out what the current rental rate is and determine if you can get a long-term lease that will lock in the rate. One of the big afford-ability issues has been rapid and steep rental increases.

Financing. Check with your local bank. There are established loans available specifically for mobile homes. These extend for as long as 15 years and the interest rates are comparable to home mortgages.

Negotiate the Price and Terms. Remember, everything in real estate, even when that real estate is mobile, is negotiable! With mobile homes, as with stick-built houses, you can lowball. However, often a better tact is to pay close to full price and insist the seller carry the financing.

Most mobile homes are owned free and clear. (Only about 15 per-cent of conventional homes are owned free and clear.) That means that the sellers are often capable, if they so choose, to carry back the mortgage themselves.

This can be a tremendous boon to you. Seller financing has virtu-ally no costs to you (including no points), has few credit require-ments, and is instantaneous. Often the seller may only require that you put 20 percent down. You could close the deal in a few days!

TIP

Be sure you get good title to the mobile home. This is often in the form of a "pink slip," similar to that for an automobile! Check it out with the Department of Motor Vehicles to be sure it's legitimate.

Why would a seller want to give you financing instead of demand-ing all cash for the sale?

Simple. Many of the owners are retirees. Often they are only mov-ing to another park or sometimes to an assisted-living situation. They may have more need of monthly income than cash. And a loan payable to them can yield a far higher interest rate than they can get at a bank or from a CD (certificate of deposit).

You may ultimately decide that a mobile home is simply not your cup of tea. However, when affordability is a big issue, you owe it to yourself to at least give it fair consideration.

CONDO, CO-OP, AND PREFAB ALTERNATIVES QUIZ

	YES	NO
1. Condos are similar to single-family homes in that you pay property taxes?	[ ]	[ ]
2. You should check out a "shared lifestyle" before buying?	[ ]	[ ]
3. There's usually less privacy in a condo or co-op?	[ ]	[ ]
4. Condos and co-ops are usually cheaper per square foot?	[ ]	[ ]
5. Condos have an HOA, co-ops have a Board?	[ ]	[ ]
6. You lose no privacy in a condo or co-op?	[ ]	[ ]
7. Noise is rarely a problem?	[ ]	[ ]
8. A townhouse is a separate type of ownership?	[ ]	[ ]
9. Location within the development is rarely a concern?	[ ]	[ ]
10. You should pay attention to how many units are rented?	[ ]	[ ]
11. Reserves are of minor importance?	[ ]	[ ]
12. Lawsuits rarely occur in condos?	[ ]	[ ]
13. Rules are difficult to change in condos and co-ops?	[ ]	[ ]
14. You can make both rent and loan payments in a mobile home?	[ ]	[ ]
15. The biggest problem with mobile homes usually is finding an available space?	[ ]	[ ]

ANSWERS

1. Yes	6. No	11. No
2. Yes	7. No	12. No
3. Yes	8. No	13. Yes
4. Yes	9. No	14. Yes
5. Yes	10. Yes	15. Yes

SCORE

12–15 Try a condo, co-op, or mobile home—you may like it!

8–11 Spend a little more time learning the differences.

5–7　You need to visit them to see what they're really like.

0-4　Stick with a single-family home!

6
Buying from a FSBO Seller

Real estate has one of the highest transaction costs of any investment. In a typical deal, for both buyer and seller combined, these costs can easily be as much as 10 to 14 percent of the sales price. On a $200,000 home, that's an amazing $20,000 to $28,000!

Anytime you can shave some of these high, usually cash, costs off the deal, it will go a long way toward making the property more affordable for you. For example, as a buyer, your closing costs (consisting of title insurance, escrow charges, and loan fees) on a $200,000 property could easily be $4,000 to $8,000. If you could get a seller to somehow pay some or most of those, that's a lot less cash you'd need to come up with. We'll see why a FSBO (For Sale By Owner) seller might be willing to do this.

Alternatively, if the seller was not using an agent and was willing to reduce the price by the typical 6 percent commission, that's $12,000 less you would have to pay for that $200,000 home.

All of which is to say that if you buy your home directly from the seller, and not use an agent, there's the potential for saving a lot of money and getting a much more affordable deal. Here's how it's done.

What the Heck Is a FSBO?

For Sale By Owner are simply words that describe a seller who's going it alone without an agent.

Why would a seller not use the convenience and expertise of an agent? The usual answer is to save money. While there is no set commission rate, most agents charge 6 percent. If a seller can avoid paying a commission, that's a saving of $18,000 on a $300,000 property. That's serious money.

Of course, most FSBO sellers overlook the fact that buyers are reluctant to deal directly with sellers. After all, how do you know the seller understands what he or she is doing? Then there's the matter of the paperwork. And how do you handle negotiations directly with no middleperson to carry the ball for you?

Thus, 85 percent of sellers who start out trying to sell FSBO eventually give up and sell using an agent. What we're concerned with here are that remaining 15 percent—the enlightened few.

What these few FSBO sellers recognize is the fact that time is money. It's not saving the commission that counts. It's getting the home sold immediately. So what they do is to give, in effect, that 6 percent (or most of it) to the buyer. In so doing, they make their home more affordable and get a very quick sale.

How Do I Find a FSBO Seller Who'll "Give Me the Commission"?

As with most things in life, you just ask!

It's done in two ways. The first is in a lowered price.

The Reduced Price

Let's assume you've done your homework and checked out the homes in a neighborhood (see Chapter 4 on farming), and you know that a particular model should sell for $200,000 since that's what recent models have sold for.

Now you find a FSBO seller in the neighborhood and you talk to this person. You immediately sense that she is an enlightened seller. She tells you that she knows homes like hers in the area go for $200,000. However, she's selling by owner and realizes that's a harder sell. So she'll cut the price by an amount equal to half the commission, or $6,000, if you'll buy quickly.

Right off the top, you're offered half the value of the commission in a price reduction. Now it's a matter of negotiation. You point out that, yes, you're willing to buy. But since there's no agent, you've got to do all the usual work that the broker performs. Plus, you've got the risks of dealing directly with a seller. You want a price reduction equal to the full commission.

The FSBO seller balks, so maybe you compromise somewhere in between. Or maybe she agrees. Remember, she's keeping her eye on the donut and not the hole. She wants the sale.

Now you've got the home at a lesser, more affordable price.

Seller-Paid Closing Costs

On the other hand, let's say that your problem is coming up with cash. You don't have the $6,000 in cash you need for your closing costs. (And you can't qualify for one of those amazing 103 percent mortgages.)

Now you present the seller with a different deal. You'll pay the full price (or whatever negotiated price you arrive at) and the seller will pay $6,000 of your closing costs.

Simple. But you may be asking yourself, can the seller pay the buyer's closing costs?

Yes and no. Yes, in that there's no law against it. No, in that some lenders will not allow the seller to pay all of the buyer's closing, but may limit them only to "nonrecurring costs."

TIP

"Nonrecurring" closings costs are those that only occur once. They may include some points, escrow charges, title fees, and other charges.

Why would a seller pay your closing costs? Why not? It should make no difference to the seller whether she knocks $6,000 off the price or keeps the price the same and pays $6,000 of your closing costs. Either way, it's $6,000 less that she receives.

Does it really work that way? You bet it does! All that you need do is negotiate with the seller and be sure that the correct price and how much of your costs he or she will pay are included in the purchase agreement.

Which brings up another point. How do you handle the paperwork when dealing with a FSBO seller?

How Do You Handle Paperwork in a FSBO Deal?

The obvious answer is, "Very carefully!"

This is an area that tolerates no mistakes. The wrong language, a misinterpretation of a law, the failure to include some important item—such as your demand for a professional home inspection—could result in a bad deal that might end up in litigation. You want it done right.

In actuality, an enlightened FSBO seller already will have considered this problem and come up with a viable solution. That solution, usually, is to have an agent prepare the purchase agreement, disclosures, and other paperwork on a fee-for-service basis. Alternatively, the seller may have an attorney do it.

TIP

The usual price for having a real estate attorney handle all the paperwork in a typical transaction is between $750 and $1,500. Today, the many new fee-for-service agents charge similar amounts. Keep in mind, however, that while attorneys who handle real estate transactions are found all over the East Coast, they are seldom found in other parts of the country. Fee-for-service agents, however, are cropping up everywhere.

If the seller hasn't come up with this solution, you can come up with it yourself. Just be sure that you agree in advance on who will pay the costs of having the paperwork done.

What about Arranging for Inspections and Getting Repairs Done?

That's what the agent does. No agent? Then it's up to you or the seller.

It's a good idea to get an initial understanding between yourself and the seller on the delegation of responsibilities. The last thing you want is to think the seller is doing the footwork while, in reality, he or she thinks you're handling it. Here's a list of some of things that need to be done in any transaction and that one or the other of you will need to do in order to ensure the deal goes through.

What to Do to Close a Deal

- Open escrow
- Get financing (exclusively your job)
- Clear title (exclusively seller's job)
- Get a professional home inspection
- Read the inspection report and negotiate any repairs
- Get a termite and pest report
- Pay for repairs to get a clearance (usually the seller's responsibility)
- Prepare a disclosure statement (seller's duty)
- Read and accept or reject disclosures (your duty—be sure you take them to a good agent to learn if all state and federal disclosure laws have been met)
- Negotiate repairs or money discount based on inspection and disclosures
- Get title insurance for both you and, if needed, the lender
- Arrange a final walk through (so you can be sure the seller hasn't damaged property during the escrow process)
- Make sure the seller moves out on time
- Make sure lender funds your financing
- Get key
- Move in

If this seems like a lot, that's because there really is a fair amount involved. However, if you and the seller split the workload, there's not really that much. And if you have a fee-for-service agent waiting in the wings to handle any problems, it should go fairly well.

How Do I Negotiate with the FSBO Seller?

This, of course, is usually the biggest problem in a FSBO deal and we've glossed over it until now. The thought of face-to-face negotiations is something that makes most of us cringe. Yet, to get a home at an affordable price by buying from a FSBO seller, it's something you'll have to do. Here are some helpful points to remember.

Negotiating Tactics

1. *Never Argue.* Always remember that if you argue with the seller, there's no third party to settle the argument. You could each end up in a rigid, uncompromising position that would make consummating a deal impossible.

   Instead, simply listen to the seller and then present your position. If you're at odds, then look for common ground and whittle away until you're both in agreement. Sound easier than it is? Perhaps, but with a little practice and keeping a cool head, it works surprisingly well.

2. *Never Get Personal.* Remember, this is business. Don't invest yourself personally. Whether or not you get the property is not an ego thing. Getting the best possible deal is simply to your advantage. As a result, never say anything personally disparaging to the seller. To do so will almost immediately end the negotiations. If the seller says something personal against you, make note of it, and then move on. If you hold it personally against the seller, again the deal's off.

3. *Don't Try to Make the Seller Like You, but It Helps If He or She Does!* Nobody wants to deal with a stranger. We all want to deal with friends, people we believe we can trust. Sellers are no different. If the seller likes you, you've got a better chance of making the deal. On the other hand, if you try to make the seller like you, chances are he or she will see through your strategy and see you as a shallow person. Not a good thing. Just be yourself. If the seller happens to like you, all the better.

4. *Never Tell a Lie.* Not even a tiny, little, small one. If you have a credit problem, you don't necessarily have to bring it up. (Although, if it's going to affect the deal, getting it out in the open early on is a good idea.) However, once it comes up, don't lie about it. Don't make it bigger than it is, but don't make it smaller either.

   Lies, even small ones, have a way of poisoning the negotiation. If the seller catches you in a lie, he or she begins wondering what else you're lying about. Maybe your whole presentation is a lie? Maybe you're just there to cheat the seller? Maybe you really don't have the cash to buy or can't qualify for the mortgage. And on and on. Telling the truth may hurt, but it hurts a lot less than lying.

5. *If the Sellers Are Unrealistic, Tell Them They Are.* This is probably the hardest rule to follow. Sellers often have inflated ideas of what their property is worth. You may know it's only worth $180,000. But they may be convinced it's actually worth $210,000. When you suggest the figure may be a bit high, they point out all the money, sweat, and time they put into it. They begin suggesting that there's something wrong with you for not realizing how good a deal it is at $210,000.

Be polite, but simply tell the sellers they're being unrealistic. Hopefully, you've done your homework and have a list of recent comparable sales to point to. Let the facts do the work for you. Simply begin reading down the list. The property on Hazel Street sold for $182,000 last month. Four months ago, the property on Downey Street sold for $178,000. Three weeks ago, escrow closed on a property just like theirs for $180,000 on the button. Figures don't lie. They tell what the house is worth.

If you tell the sellers they are unrealistic and back it up, one of two things will happen. Either, they'll agree and you'll have a deal at a price you can afford. Or, they'll simply reject what you say and throw you out, which is okay because at least you'll have saved yourself from wasting any more time on a hopeless negotiation.

What Do I Do Once We're Agreed?

Get it in writing. Agreement is a fleeting thing. You may agree on Wednesday evening, but by Thursday morning the seller may be having second thoughts and may want to start negotiations all over again.

Get yourself immediately down to an attorney or agent who'll write up the deal, and then get everyone's signature. Only then can you breathe a conditional sigh of relief (conditioned on the deal finally closing some 30 days later after you get financing, the seller clears title, and everything else goes according to plan).

Where Do I Find FSBO Sellers?

If I've sold you on the idea of trying to buy a home from a FSBO sell-er, then it's time to go looking. In Chapter 4 we talked about farm-ing an area. That's your first source of FSBOs. They will turn up occasionally in every neighborhood.

Also, check the local newspapers under the head, "For Sale By Owner." Sometimes there will be many ads there; sometimes only a few. If any are in your price range and located where you want to buy, call them right up and get out there to look at the property.

Also check the Internet. I've not listed any FSBO sites because they come and go with surprising frequency. Simply use a good search engine to locate them. But don't be hesitant to check out any properties you find there. Usually the seller's name and phone num-ber are listed. Just call him or her up and continue on as if you had seen the ad in the paper.

TRAP

Remember that the Internet is worldwide. Be sure that a property you find is, in fact, in a location where you want to buy. It could be in the next town or the next continent!

How Do I Introduce Myself to a FSBO Seller?

We've come full circle. When it's time to visit a FSBO seller, you have to make nice. Unlike when you're touring with an agent, when you can wear whatever you want and act anyway you like, when you first meet a FSBO seller, you must be on your best behavior.

Dress well. Be polite. Don't hog the conversation. Let the FSBO seller give you a tour of the property. Add the complimentary "oohs" and "aahs" at the usual places. In other words, try to make a good impression. Remember, if it turns out that this is the place you want to buy, this seller is the person with whom you're going to negotiate and with whom you're going to take the sales journey.

TIP

I recommend that you don't begin negotiations on your first visit. Rather, use that as strictly an exploratory mission. Try to find out as much about the property and the seller's motivation as you can. At the same time, the seller will be trying to assess you and your intentions. Later, after you've left and had a chance to think about it, if you like the place, call the seller and arrange another time to come down and negotiate. Waiting has the added effect of letting the seller know you're not too anxious. And calling for an appointment allows the seller to build anticipation as to what you might have on your mind and how much you might offer. It gets the seller more interested in seeing what you've got to offer.

Spend Time

Don't plan on simply breezing in, making an offer, and then breezing out. Plan to spend time, hours if necessary. Use "small talk." Get to know the sellers better. Let them get to know you.

When you present your offer, present it one element at a time. Sometimes, if you're lowballing, it's better to present favorable terms first with the price last.

Drag things out. The more time you and the seller spend together, the more likely you are both to be committed to working out a deal. After all, no one likes to "waste" an entire evening with nothing to show for it. After a while, the seller will begin bending over backwards to "save" the deal.

For more techniques on negotiating, check out my book *Tips and Traps When Negotiating Real Estate* (McGraw-Hill, 1999).

Should I Really Try Buying from a FSBO Seller?

We've seen how it can save you money and make a home more affordable. We've seen how it can save you cash when you are strapped for cash. So, yes of course, if you can find a FSBO that's suitable, certainly try to make a deal out of it.

However, just as 85 percent of all FSBO sellers never actually do a deal and eventually list, so too, 85 percent of all buyers never purchase from a FSBO seller, but instead go through an agent.

It's understandable. For most of us, direct negotiations, particularly in an area like real estate that can seem arcane, can simply be too hard. If you decide against it, don't worry. I'll understand. But if it's a good FSBO deal, don't let it go. Contact an agent and have them negotiate for you.

Will an Agent Really Negotiate with a FSBO Seller?

Certainly, for a commission. Usually the agent will get the FSBO seller to pop for the commission. But if not, be aware that you might have to pay for the agent's work. In that case, you might need to reevaluate just how affordable a deal it really is.

Almost any agent can act as a "buyer's agent" for you. But, as noted, just be sure you have an understanding up front as to how much the agent will charge and who will be responsible for paying the fee. It would be a shame to let a terrific deal go just for want of a negotiator. And there are nearly a million agents nationwide just waiting for the chance to serve you!

For more information on buying a FSBO, check out my book *The For Sale By Owner Kit*, Fourth Edition (Dearborn, 2002).

FSBO QUIZ

	YES	NO
1. FSBO means "for sale by owner?"	[ ]	[ ]
2. Nearly half of all FSBO sellers sell their own home?	[ ]	[ ]
3. Some FSBO sellers will split the commission they save with you?	[ ]	[ ]
4. It's better to not let the FSBO seller handle the paperwork?	[ ]	[ ]

	YES	NO
5. With a FSBO, you and the seller have to do all the legwork to close the deal?	[ ]	[ ]
6. It pays to get personal when arguing with a FSBO seller?	[ ]	[ ]
7. White lies sometimes help clinch a deal?	[ ]	[ ]
8. You have to make a FSBO seller become realistic about price?	[ ]	[ ]
9. FSBOs are only on the Internet?	[ ]	[ ]
10. An agent will never negotiate with a FSBO seller?	[ ]	[ ]

ANSWERS

1. Yes   6. No

2. No   7. No

3. Yes   8. Yes

4. Yes   9. No

5. Yes   10. No

SCORING

8–10   You're ready to deal directly with sellers.

4–7   Look, but be wary.

1–3   Deal only with agents.

7

Cutting Costs with Fixer-Uppers

One of the most widely accepted methods of getting into a home at a lower price is to buy one that's run-down and then fix it up. These are called "fixer-uppers" or sometimes on the East Coast, "handyman specials." Because of their poor condition, they are bargain priced.

But how much more affordable are fixers really?

That depends. Every home is different. However, I have seen people buy fixers at 50 percent of the cost of comparable homes in good shape. And I've also seen them buy fixers at only about 5 percent off. As I said, every situation is different.

What's important, however, is that you often can buy into a good neighborhood and get a basically good home you could otherwise not get, if you're willing to put some "sweat equity" into it.

What's Involved in Buying a Fixer?

The whole idea here is that you get a lower price because the house is in bad shape and you personally spend time and effort putting it back into shape. Rather than spend money on the house, you spend "sweat" and, thus, get it for a more affordable price.

If you're the sort who doesn't like working up a sweat or doing work around the house, then stay away from fixers. These are properties that need lots of TLC, and sometimes more. To make them more affordable, they will require you to get in there and get your hands dirty. You'll find yourself painting, cleaning, hammering, and oh so much more! They will occupy a substantial part of your time for at least a few months until you get them whipped into shape. Working on a fixer can be a drain on an otherwise active lifestyle.

On the other hand, most people I know who have bought fixers say it was one of the best experiences of their life. Indeed, some couples say working on the house helped bring their marriage together! I've done more fixers than I care to count, and I've always had an enjoyable experience. I think it's because you get a sense of accomplishment from putting something back into shape that was run-down. And very possibly making it even better than new!

Beyond the emotional and time involvement, however, there's also a complex financial commitment involved with doing a fixer. Not only do you have to come up with the cash and financing to buy a home, but you also have to come up with the money to fix it up after you've bought it. In addition, you often need to come up with another place to live while you're doing the work. You can't always count on being able to live in the fixer while you're doing the work.

If you have some available cash, then you may want to consider a fixer. If you're cash poor, however, then a fixer may not be the best route for you to take.

How Much Cash Is Involved?

That's hard to say since, as noted, each case is different. However, in all cases you will need money in two distinct time frames. You'll first need cash to make the initial purchase. And later you'll need additional cash to pay for labor and materials during the fix-up period. How you structure your financing to get this cash will largely determine your success or failure in the project.

If you have a lot of cash on hand, then there is simply no problem. You'll just spend it from your own account. However, I'm assuming you're like the rest of us and that cash is scarce. (Why else read this book!). So the real question becomes, how can you get somebody else to finance most of the costs?

Here are some financing generalities that will be true for most fixers.

1. *You Won't Be Able to Get as High an Initial Loan Amount.* This only makes sense. Lenders aren't going to be eager to give you a high LTV (loan to value) on a property that's not in prime shape. If

you didn't make your payments and the lender had to take the property back, the lender would be stuck with a property it might only be able to sell at a loss.

Rather, lenders are going to give you low LTVs. You can expect the highest mortgage you're likely to get will be in the 80 percent range. And having lenders tell you that they'll loan a maximum of 70 percent or even 60 percent is not uncommon.

2. *You May Be Able to Get a Construction-Type Loan.* On the other hand, lenders are no dummies. They realize that once you've completed your renovation work, the place will be worth considerably more. Hence, they are often willing to give you a mortgage that is ultimately based on the eventual fixed-up value. However, they won't give you all of the money until you've completed the work. But they may give you partial payments along the way. Here's a typical example:

LTV when you buy 75%	$150,000
LTV when fixed up 95%	$190,000
Additional payment(s) to you	$ 40,000

As you can see, when you buy you get a much smaller LTV. However, the LTV expands when you complete the work.

TRAP

It's important that you arrange for all your financing before you buy. If you wait until you are the owner of the property and have started work, it may be impossible to get any additional needed financing until you've finished. The reason is that lenders are hesitant to advance money once construction has begun for fear the repayment of their loan will become secondary to mechanic's liens. [Mechanic's liens are a technical subject. For a discussion, check out my book *Tips & Traps When Renovating Your Home* (McGraw-Hill, 2000).]

1. *You May Be Able to Get the Seller to Help.* From the previous discussion, it would appear that you'd need huge amounts of cash to buy the fixer. However, there are ways around this. The most common is to get the seller to help with the financing.

Often the seller on a fixer wants desperately to get out. If you offer an exit for him or her, but condition it on the seller providing some financing for say 6 months to 1 year, he or she very likely might accept it. Here, the seller agrees to hold paper (a second mortgage) without receiving payments until you've done the work. Then, with the work done and the place fixed up, you refinance (or get your payoff as noted above) and pay the seller. If you play your cards right, you can sometimes make the purchase with little to no money of your own in the deal!

TIP

Sometimes the seller is a lender who has taken the property back through foreclosure. Here, the lender may be more inclined to give you a construction-type loan. In some cases, the lender may provide both primary and secondary financing on the same property just to be rid of it!

2. *You May Be Able to Get Short-Term Financing.* Remember, the money you need for fixing up the place is short term. Once it's fixed up you can refinance and get this money back. You might only need it for 6 months or perhaps less.

   That means there are all sorts of avenues open to you. You can borrow it from relatives or friends. You can get cash advances on your credit cards. (Visa and MasterCard have financed more than a few fixer-uppers!) You can even get home improvement loans from banks.

What about the Timing?

From the above discussion, it should be clear that financing for fixers is available. Indeed, if you ultimately end up with a very high LTV, say 95 percent or higher, your cash involvement may be minimal.

However, the problem is that at certain points during the fixing-up process you will be in need of cash. And if it's not available just when you need it, you might not be able to successfully complete the deal.

Critical Times When You Will Need Cash

1. When you buy—for down payment and closing costs
2. When you begin the work—for labor and materials
3. Half way through the work—for labor and materials
4. When the work is complete—for labor and materials

Note that the need for cash occurs many different times during the fixing-up process.

TRAP

Don't make the mistake of thinking you need all of your refurbishing money up front. You'll need it doled out a little at a time. And that can be maddening. If you're putting in a kitchen you'll need funds to fix the floor, walls, and ceiling. Only when that's done will you need funds for cabinets and countertops. Only when they are completed will you need the funds for appliances, fixtures, and flooring. You don't need your cash all at once. You need it doled out.

What should be apparent is that one of the keys to success in doing a fixer-upper is knowing when you'll need funds and having them ready at the appropriate time. To help you determine your potential needs, use the list at the end of this chapter.

How Do I Find a Fixer?

Fixer-uppers abound in all communities everywhere in the country. They exist for a wide variety of reasons. These include:

- Owners who simply never maintain or repair their home
- Owners who abandon their property
- Owners who lose their property to foreclosure
- Owners who have older homes that have simply decayed

The trick is identifying a fixer that has potential and avoiding those that are simply hopeless.

Work with Agents

If affordability is an issue with you and you're willing to dig in and try your hand at a fixer, be sure you let your real estate agent know. Agents are always on the lookout for fixers, and if they know that's what you want, they'll look for you.

TRAP

Don't expect agents to fall down at your feet if you tell them you specifically want a fixer. Agents know that good fixers are difficult to find and completing a deal on them often takes lots more work than selling a fixed-up house. About the best response you're likely to get is to have the agent show you any even remotely acceptable properties and then say he or she will call if and when something more suitable shows up.

Work the MLS

Be sure you scout out what's currently available on the MLS (Multiple Listing Service) with your agent. This can take time and careful looking. The MLS is available on computer in almost all areas of the country. Simply sit down with your agent and use the listing's search engine to try and discover suitable properties.

For example, you can pull the lowest-priced properties in each neighborhood and then read the listings carefully, looking for clues that you have a fixer. Expressions on the listing such as, "This baby needs tender loving care" or "sweat equity opportunity" are almost sure indications that you're looking at a fixer listing. Check for other clues that the listing agent wrote that suggests this house is a fixer.

Also, carefully peruse the picture. Almost all listings today come with at least one good color image. Does the house look dazzling as many a fixed-up place will? Or does it look a little tired? Check especially for tall weeds in the front yard, big cracks in the driveway, and temporary cyclone fences. All indicate a problem house.

TIP

Look for listings that are aged. The longer a house has been on the market, the more likely that it has problems. Besides, sellers of homes that have just been listed are unlikely to consider taking price cuts. Usually a seller won't want to reduce the price until a home has sat unsold for a minimum of 30 days and often 60.

Your agent can also be a big help if he or she knows the area well. The agent can read the listing and look at the picture and say something like, "I saw that house when it was listed last year. It's come down considerably in price. It shows very badly. I'm not surprised it didn't sell."

Words such as these should be music to your ears. They indicate that the property is very likely a fixer.

TIP

In real estate, appearance is critical. Properties that look good and show well sell quickly, often for higher prices than you would expect. Properties that show badly, often called "dogs," take a long time to sell and command lower prices. If you're looking for a fixer, you only want to look at the dogs.

TRAP

Beware of falling for good-looking properties. We're all human, and when we see a home that shows very well, we're just as likely to fall for it as the next person. However, keep yourself focused. You're looking for the run-down homes. You want property that shows badly. Just keep telling yourself how nice that decayed old dog will turn out *after* you buy it for next to nothing and fix it up!

Be sure you go through *all* of the current listings. This could take time. If you're in a metropolitan area that has thousands of listings, it could take days. Spend the time. It will be worth it.

Once you've identified the properties you think are fixers, have your agent call the listing broker and ask if it is indeed a fixer. Or did you simply read the listing wrong? The listing broker should immediately be able to let you know.

If the lister says it's a dog, get your agent to show it to you. Don't just drive by. Often first appearances can be deceptive. Go inside. See exactly what the problems are with the house.

If it's definitely a dog, identify the problem and see if it's something you want to tackle (see the next section). If it's simply a home where the owner has yet to do some painting and cleaning, move on.

Check the Expireds

If you don't find anything suitable with the current listings, ask to see those listing that have expired. The MLS also carries information on listings that have expired without being sold. This can be a real treasure trove.

Listings that have expired are no longer listed for sale. However, the owners often are still willing to sell them. It's just that they've gotten discouraged and have taken the home off the market, often just temporarily.

You have to ask yourself, why did the listing expire? If it was a sharp house, it should have sold unless the price was unrealistic. Often the reason a home didn't sell is because it's a fixer.

TIP

Your agent should be thrilled to go over the expired listings with you. If you find one you like, the agent has a chance to get both the listing and selling commission on it. In other words, he or she can make twice as much as on a house listed by someone else. However, be aware that there are certain rules that agents abide by. For example, some will not try to list an expired until at least 30 days has passed to allow the previous lister a chance to relist. Whatever the rules, just be sure if it's a good property that, one way or another, you see it and get the chance to make an offer.

Check the FSBOs

We've already discussed FSBOs in Chapter 6. If you can't find anything suitable working with your agent, farm a neighborhood or two looking for FSBOs. Sometimes you'll come across an FSBO that's a real dog. The seller hasn't listed simply because it shows so bad. It could be perfect for you.

Pass Out Flyers

I've done this many times, and it can produce results. Put together a nice, small flyer (perhaps on a 4-by-6 card) saying that you want to move into the area and are looking for a home that you can buy and fix up. Put only your telephone number. And drop it off at every house in the neighborhood. There's no telling how many, if any, calls you'll get or where they'll lead. However, unless you let people know that you're looking, you'll never come across someone who wants to sell but just hasn't yet listed or tried going FSBO.

Check Out Newspapers, Internet, Postings

There may be sellers out there that want to tell you they've got the perfect fixer. Maybe they've taken an ad in the local newspaper. Perhaps they've put the home on a Web site, maybe even their own. Or perhaps they've written it up on a 4-by-6 card and posted it at a local grocery or drugstore.

Where you get the information is irrelevant. I once bought a fixer after meeting the relative of a seller who was sitting next to me on a plane ride between Oakland and Los Angeles! We got to talking and she told me about the house. I made arrangements to see the property and liked it. The seller and I agreed on price, and within 30 days I owned it!

How Do I Evaluate a Fixer?

Once you've found it, the next question you must answer is: "How much work is required?" That's a lot harder to do than it may seem at first.

Fixers run the gamut of those that simply need superficial work to those in such bad shape they need to be scrapped and a new house erected from scratch.

Most of us would prefer to stay closer to the superficial realm where cleaning, painting, and replacing fixtures is about the most we'd be called upon to do. The problem is that the discount on superficial fixers is often so small as to make them simply not worthwhile considering.

For example, let's say that a home in good condition would sell for $250,000. However, this home badly needs paint inside and out. Screens on windows need to be replaced. Doors have holes in them and need to be repaired or replaced. The carpeting is in terrible shape and new carpeting is needed. And the yard needs to be completely landscaped. Let's say you go through this superficially challenged home and come up with the following figures:

Cost of Repairs for Superficial Fixer

Paint outside	$ 2,500
Paint inside	3,000
New wall-to-wall carpeting	6,000
New screens on windows	500
New fixtures	2,000
New appliances	2,500
Landscaping	5,000
Total cost of fixing	$21,500

You figure the total costs for fixing up the property would be a little over $21,000. Plus, of course, the effort and time spent, at least another $5,000 at minimum. Thus, the price of the property should be no more than $224,500.

My guess is that the sellers are asking perhaps $245,000 for the home, just $5,000 off what it should sell for in prime shape. Yes, the sellers will acknowledge the home needs work, but when asked will say something such as, "It's just superficial, a little paint, a little cleaning. We've knocked five grand off the price to cover it."

Almost never will a seller "fess up" and acknowledge the true costs of the superficial work that a home needs. And if push comes to shove and the house doesn't sell, such sellers will often get a quick home improvement loan on the property and use the money to slap on some paint, put in cheap carpeting, fixtures, and appliances. Then they will try to sell it for more than market value—perhaps $260,000 in our example.

All of which is to say that while the superficial fixer may be ideal for the person who is trying to do a fixer-upper for the first time, it is also the hardest property to get a good deal on.

TRAP

There is an apparent contradiction in the fact that the house that looks the worst, a superficial fixer, often costs the most. The trouble arises from the fact that today sellers are sophisticated enough to know that superficial fixes are cheap and easy and they simply don't want to give up any of their profits because of them.

Look for More Serious Problems

Once we get past the superficial fixer, the problems quickly escalate from the simply bad to the truly terrible.

At the upper end are homes that have broken foundations, that have collapsing roofs, that have been condemned because of fires or ground shifting, that are sliding down hills, and on and on. Homes that have problems as serious as this often don't look that bad, but they are. And they are usually the least expensive. Indeed, you may be able to pick up the property for just the cost of the land. In some cases, that's less than half the price for a home in good condition.

Nevertheless, I strongly recommend that you stay away from such calamitous problems. While all of the above are fixers, and I have worked on many such situations, they require a background in construction with lots of experience. If you're doing this the first time out, you could get burned badly on one of them.

Rather, what you want is something in between the calamity and the superficial fixer. You want a home that has a serious problem, but one which you can deal with and have a reasonable chance of success. Of course, make sure you get a thorough home inspection before buying any fixer.

As I said, fixers are on a case-by-case basis and it all depends on what you turn up. But here are some examples I have either worked on or known about.

Typical First-Time Fixers

- *Fire Damaged Home.* No structural damage, but lots of smoke and cracked drywall. Needs to be drywalled, taped, textured with new flooring, paint, fixtures, and so on.
- *Cracked Slab.* Steel rebars intact, but cracked cement. Usually requires cosmetic fix to floors plus extensive drainage system to prevent further damage.
- *Peeling, Leaking Roof.* Found in high temperatures in the Southwest, requires reinsulating attic and reroofing with higher-quality materials, plus painting and cleaning up water damage.
- *Water in Basement.* No serious damage to foundation. Requires sump pump to keep area dry and refurbishing of basement.
- *Galvanized Piping with Multiple Leaks.* Often requires redoing entire house with copper plumbing. Then fixing up all the leaks. Costs $5,000 to $10,000 for a pro to do it.
- *Inoperative Septic Tank.* With no problem to leach field, may require installing new septic tank and cleaning up all fecal material. If leach field is damaged, there must be room for a new field or else the problem may not be solvable!

Note that in each of these cases there's both a serious problem and a superficial problem. Typically the serious problem causes damage that results in the need for cosmetic work. However, the serious problem means that the seller cannot simply dismiss it.

Note also that the problem and remedy are challenging. It's not easy. That's the reason that the seller doesn't correct it himself or herself. That's also the reason that you must be willing to take on a hard project.

TIP

Perhaps the most important thing you can do when evaluating a fixer is to determine whether you can do the work yourself, or whether it's beyond you.

For this reason, it's always a good idea to call in experts—contractors, engineers, agents—people who specialize in fixing the particular problem. In many cases they'll simply give you a bid. In others, you may have to pay them a fee for their analysis. But either way, very often only they can tell you how the problem can be correctly fixed. And how much that will cost.

How Do I Know How Much to Offer for a Fixer?

In theory, the answer is quite simple. You simply subtract the cost of fixing up the house, plus what you feel your time is worth and a profit from what the house should sell for in perfect condition. And that's how much to offer. For example:

Basic Formula for Making an Offer

Value if in perfect shape	$150,000
Less cost of fixing up	−50,000
Less your time and effort	−25,000
Your offer	$ 75,000

Note that in our example, the offer is actually about 50 percent of the value of the property in good shape. Often this is the case. A true fixer will usually cost a lot of money to put back into shape. While this makes the property more affordable initially, remember that you still have to put it back into good shape!

TIP

The cost depends on whether you hire it all out, or whether you do much of it yourself. My suggestion is that when determining how much to offer, you always base this on hiring everything out. That way, in case you err, you'll at least not be erring on the side of paying too much. If you later do much, if not all, of the work yourself, your savings will be that much more.

Also note how affordable the house becomes when it's a fixer. You get it at a bargain-basement price. Of course, that's because you're putting in sweat equity.

Once again, when you do this be sure of your numbers. As noted above, call in experts to tell you what the costs will be. If this is your first time, you're very likely to be far off on your own estimates.

Don't Overestimate What You Can Do

I once had a friend who bought a fixer that needed a new roof. He told himself that he could do that.

However, after he bought the home and began ripping off the old roof, he discovered rot in the roof beams. They needed to be replaced. "I can do that," he told himself.

He slowly took down the roof beams. In the process, however, he stepped between the rafters and fell through the Sheetrock into the living room, breaking his leg.

At this stage, the house had no roof and a rather big hole in the living room ceiling. And one thing was certain, he could do no more. At that point he had to hire professionals to come in and finish the job. It ended up costing him far more than he had anticipated.

The moral here is that you need to know your limits. We all can do miraculous things, but we all have limits as to what we can accomplish.

How do you know what you can do?

The answer usually comes from experience. If you're a roofer by trade, then when you say you can handle a roof I'm a believer. However, if you're an accountant by trade, I'm a disbeliever until I see otherwise.

On the other hand, maybe you're an accountant who has worked with his dad in construction. You've hammered on roofs before. Now I'm more of a believer.

If you're a "handyman" who has done a lot of things around the house and who has been involved in construction, chances are you can do most any fixing up you set your mind to. If, however, you really can't hammer a nail in straight and don't know a Phillip's head from a crowbar, maybe you'd be better off hiring it out.

How Do I Get the Seller to Accept My Offer?

That's the rub.

With the exception of the recession of the early 1990s, the direction of real estate for the past 60 years has been almost straight up. Everyone knows how valuable property is. Everyone knows how prices have soared. And no one, particularly not the seller you're dealing with, wants to sell for less than the highest price any house similar to his or hers sold for in the past 3 years.

Thus, getting a seller to accept a reasonable price for a fixer is almost always going to be a difficult process. The seller will typically refuse to see how much the property is worth and will want more. This makes your job all the more challenging.

There are two strategies that I've found helpful in getting sellers to accept my offers. The first is to lay it all out so that the seller sees exactly where I'm coming from.

The second is to play the numbers game. If this seller doesn't want to do a realistic deal, move on. There's no shortage of home sellers.

Laying out the Deal

When offers are presented to sellers, typically the agents do it without the buyer present. This is a nice tradition in which the agent's (presumably strong) negotiating skills work in the buyer's favor. Not so, however, in a fixer. Here my suggestion is that you go with the agent to explain exactly what you have in mind. Don't rely on the agent to explain how you plan to fix up the property. (Of course, if you're buying directly from a FSBO seller or a bank, there's no problem—you'll represent yourself.)

TRAP

Some agents will try to tell you that you're not allowed to be there when the offer is presented. Nonsense. There's no law that says the buyer can't present the offer. What the agents mean is that in most cases the buyers get in the way. They get emotional. And the agents lose the advantage of being independent third parties. However, when it's a true fixer you need to be there.

My suggestion is that you present the offer in the following steps:

Steps to Presenting an Offer on a Fixer

1. Indicate to the seller what the home would be worth if it were in perfect shape. You can do this by coming up with comps for similar homes sold over the past 6 months to a year. Any agent worth his salt should be able to come up with these for you within a few minutes. Try to get the seller to agree with you. Since this price is probably more than the seller's asking price, given the home's current bad shape, you shouldn't have much of a problem here.

2. Indicate what the problems are. Having opinions from contractors, engineers, technicians, and so on will bolster your case. You're not giving your opinion here. You're dealing with facts. It may turn out that the seller didn't realize just how extensive the problems were.

3. Indicate what you propose to do to correct the problem. Again, use expert evaluations to bolster your case. And explain exactly how much it will cost.

4. Indicate that you plan to be paid for your time working on this . Indicate exactly how much that is.

5. Finally, lay out the figures just as was done in the Basic Formula for Making an Offer on page 81 and Cost of Repairs on page 78. It's at this point that the seller sees how much you're offering and sees how you arrived at the figure.

Now what are the sellers to do? They can argue with your experts, perhaps putting forth estimates of their own.

Consider what they have. Maybe their experts are better than yours. Maybe not. Now you're arguing objectively about what's wrong and how to correct it. You should be able to come to some sort of agreement if you both negotiate in good faith.

Or perhaps the sellers argue that you are asking too much for your time or your profit margin. If so, ask them what their time is worth and what they figure a reasonable profit would be. Maybe you'll agree with them! On the other hand, maybe not and no deal can be reached.

Finally, you may agree on everything, but the sellers simply don't want to sell for so little. They figure their property is simply worth a whole lot more. Their argument is strictly emotional.

Now present your own emotional case. You'd love to buy a house already fixed up and ready to go. You'd love not to have to go through the incredible hassle of a fixer-upper. But you can't afford it. In fact, this is the only way you can afford to buy a home in this neighborhood, where you want your kids to go to school and where you feel your spouse will be safe.

Now what are the sellers going to do? Why they are going to accept! Or not.

If they accept, you've done it. If they don't, it's time to move on to the next fixer without looking back.

TRAP

If the sellers are adamant and refuse to budge, even though you've shown that your figures are solid, don't change your figures. Don't offer more. To do so is the worst mistake you can make with a fixer. Most people who buy fixers pay too much. Only much later when they realize how much it costs to make the necessary repairs do they realize their mistake. Only then it's too late. If you pay too much going in, it may turn out that after you've done all the work, the house ends up costing you more than a similar house in perfect shape! Move on. There are a lot more fish in the sea.

How Do I Structure the Deal?

Everything needs to be spelled out in writing in the purchase agreement. You need to indicate the financing and that the deal is subject to your obtaining it. You need to indicate whether the seller is to provide any financing by carrying back paper. Perhaps, most important in these kinds of deals, you need to have time to conduct thorough inspections of the property to be sure that what you think is wrong with it really is and that there isn't something more. In a normal transaction, the buyer is given two weeks for inspection. You may want to demand a month.

Be sure you have a competent agent or attorney draw up the purchase agreement, including all the necessary boilerplate language to

protect you and to allow you to back out of the deal in case something goes wrong.

Once the sellers accept, don't think it's a done deal. Now you have
to do your due diligence by having those inspections. And you have
to get that financing you were pre-approved for. And you have to
make plans for getting the work done, including taking time off
your day job!

Can I Really Do It?

You won't know until and unless you try. However, be assured that
there are people across the country that every day are buying fixers
and are successfully doing the needed repair work.

My own feeling is that chances are you wouldn't even dream of
doing it unless you'd had some previous good experiences in building, and were confident because of those. In other words, chances
are that if you think you can, you probably can.

For more information on fixing up properties, check out my book
Tips & Traps When Renovating Your Home (McGraw-Hill, 2000).

FUNDS THAT YOU'LL NEED
TO COMPLETE YOUR
FIXER-UPPER

_____ 1. **Down Payment**—Needed for most purchases anyway.

_____ 2. **Closing Costs**—May be smaller if there's seller help
with the financing.

_____ 3. **Paid Evaluations**—For engineers, inspectors, and
others to tell you what's wrong, how to fix it, and
how much it will cost. This needn't be much, perhaps under $1,000.

_____ 4. **Tear Down**—Varies enormously depending on
what's done. From under $500 for scrapping a
kitchen to over $5,000 for walls, roof, ceiling, and
foundation.

_____   5. **Materials**—Be sure to add up *all* the materials needed to complete the job. A materials' list should be put together listing everything. Be sure your cost estimates are accurate.

_____   6. **Labor**—This is for all the work you'll hire out. As noted, be sure to include all work unless you're absolutely sure you'll do it.

_____   7. **Your Labor**—Your time is not free. Figure out what it's worth to you.

_____   8. **Your Profit**—Every entrepreneurial job should have a profit. It might be large or small. But it should be in there.

_____   9. **Transaction Costs**—Any costs involved in buying the property, such as title insurance, escrow, loan fees, etc.

_____   10. **Miscellaneous**—Include a figure to cover whatever you left out.

8

Building Your Own Home

An avenue to affordable housing that an increasing number of Americans are considering is building their own home. The savings from you doing it versus having a contractor do it range from 15 to 30 percent. When I've built homes for my family, I've found the savings to be even higher!

Building your own home is surely not for everyone. Some of the tasks, such as putting in a foundation or roof, can be daunting.

On the other hand, it's not as difficult as it may sound. At its most basic level, all we're talking about is buying a lot and then erecting a house on it. If you don't like to hammer and nail, you can hire out all the work. Just being your own contractor saves lots of money. On the other hand, if you're handy, you can do much of the actual building yourself and save even more.

Some of the most successful individual home builders that I've seen buy a small, used trailer, park it on their lot, and live in it for a year or so while they're building their home. Then they sell the trailer, recouping most of its cost! Thus, they've lived virtually rent free for a year while constructing their home.

But I'm sure many readers for whom this is something totally new are wondering: Isn't it very difficult to build a house? How do you know what to do? How do you get it right?

How Hard Is It?

It's not brain surgery. And there are experts available all along the way to step in and assist when you aren't sure exactly what to do. If you can follow a set of plans, you can build a house.

TIP

In all areas of the country, you're going to need local building department approval for both your plans and for each step of construction. While some view this as bothersome, for the first-time builder it's actually helpful. Most building departments and inspectors go out of their way to explain how things should be done to meet code. And if you do something wrong, they'll make constructive suggestions on how to most quickly, easily, and cheaply correct it.

Perhaps getting an overview of what's involved will help lay to rest unwarranted fears about home building. Here are the steps involved:

Typical Steps in Building Your Own Home
1. Arrange for financing
2. Find and buy a suitable lot
3. Obtain a complete set of building plans
4. Hire a contractor or subcontractors to work for you
5. Do the actual construction
   a. Clear the land
   b. Build the foundation
   c. Frame the home
   d. Do rough plumbing, electrical, and heating
   e. Put on the outside skin and roofing
   f. Insulate
   g. Drywall, tape, and texture
   h. Finish plumbing, electrical, and heating
   i. Finish carpentry and flooring
   j. Put in appliances and fixtures
   k. Paint
6. Get the "takeout" or permanent financing

These steps are no different than what a professional builder goes through. The only real difference is that you're doing as much or as little of it as you choose. And you're pocketing the builder's profit and usually saving a lot of the labor costs.

TRAP

Don't think you can build as cheaply as a professional. You can't because pro builders have economies of scale (they're building many houses, not just one). They have a regular crew of workers and they've done it before, so they'll tend to make fewer mistakes.

TIP

On the other hand, if you go slowly and move carefully, you can avoid most mistakes. You can frequently negotiate lower labor costs by hiring people to work "on the side," and you can buy much of what you need on sale. And you don't have to pay the builder a profit; you can pocket that money yourself.

What's important to remember is the payoff. You should be able to build for much less than you can buy. Thus, you will be able to afford more than you thought you could. If this is sufficient motivation to interest you, read on and we'll explore in greater detail how it's done.

Arrange for the Financing

I like to put this as the first step because without financing no deal can be done. However, you cannot complete the financing until you own a lot, have a complete set of plans ready to go, and can explain to a lender how you have the expertise to complete the project.

To begin, however, you can contact a lender and get pre-approved. The lender can take a look at your financials and give you a sense of how big a loan you can get.

When building, you actually get two separate loans. The first is the construction loan. The second is the "takeout" loan.

Construction Loan

Here, the lender advances you money as materials are purchased and work is completed. The loan is usually for a short time, a year or so. This is done in many stages. To give you an idea of how, here's a typical 7-step construction loan.

7-Step Construction Loan

>   Payment 1 — For building materials package
>
>   Payment 2 — When foundation is up
>
>   Payment 3 — When framing is completed
>
>   Payment 4 — When rough plumbing, heating, and electrical are finished
>
>   Payment 5 — When skin, roof, windows, and doors are finished
>
>   Payment 6 — When finish work is completed
>
>   Payment 7 — When mechanic's lien periods have run out

Of course, your lender may have many more or many fewer steps. It's important to note that payment is usually made after the work is done. Hence, you're going to need to get both labor and materials on credit, at least for a short while. This is usually not a problem.

Also note that there is no payment made, in this case, for the lot. You will usually need to arrange for the purchase of the lot separate from the construction loan. (Some construction loans will pay out when the lot is free and clear, but not usually when it's an individual doing the building.)

Takeout Loan

This is permanent financing that "takes out" the construction loan. It is the same sort of loan that you would get if you bought an already built house. Typically, you can get financing for up to 90 to 95 percent of the final value of the building. I've not seen takeouts for 100 percent or more of LTV actually put through on new construction. However, you probably can get total financing on a refi (refinancing an existing mortgage).

By going for pre-approval with a lender, you'll learn not only *if* you can get a construction loan, but what the lender's requirements are. And you'll learn how big a takeout loan you can qualify for, thus telling you how much you can afford to spend for the lot and building.

Lender's Expert Requirement

Lenders are always eager to loan—that's how they do business. However, they are also always risk averse. And in this case, they are sure to be very concerned about your ability to successfully complete construction. After all, they will be advancing you money on a regular basis through the construction loan. What if after a few months they discover that you're putting up "the house that Jack built." The work is subpar and doesn't meet acceptable building standards. They might have to step in, foreclose, and redo the home themselves at significant cost. At worst, they might lose all the money they had already invested.

To allay the lender's fears, you must be able to demonstrate your competency. If you have a contractor's license, it will help. If you can point out buildings you've successfully built before, that will also help. But chances are you won't have either of these options. So what do you do?

You hire someone who has the background to qualify for a construction loan. The easiest, though most expensive, choice is an experienced general contractor. He or she steps into your place and the lender is pleased.

However, one of the things you probably wanted to do was avoid paying a contractor's profit. So you may try to obtain a fee-for-service arrangement. The contractor will use his license and will generally oversee the construction for a set fee. However, you'll do all the work of hiring and supervising subcontractors as well as much of the physical work. The trouble is that few contractors are willing to take all the risk for someone who's basically untried.

Your next best alternative is a contractor-carpenter. Often carpenters are really wannabe builders. They may have their contractor's license, but haven't yet had the opportunity to put up many houses. They are hungry for somewhere to start. You can give them that opportunity. You make the arrangement for them to act as your contractor and to do much of the carpentry, while you do the hiring and much of the labor.

This sort of arrangement often works well for everyone involved. You (because you now have an expert on board), the lender (who now has a licensed builder), and the carpenter (who's getting a start) all benefit.

Find and Buy a Lot

Once you've arranged for financing, the next step is finding and buying a lot. Note from our discussion on financing, it's unlikely you'll be able to finance the purchase of the lot through the construction loan lender. Indeed, what most lenders would prefer is that you buy and pay off the lot with cash first!

This may or may not be possible given your financial situation and the cost of the lot.

In some rural areas, lots are available with utilities for under $10,000, which may be doable for you. On the other hand, prime lots in cities may go for $100,000 or more. The immediate question now becomes: How can you afford the lot?

The answer if you can't afford to pay cash is to have the seller finance the lot purchase. The first lot I ever bought for building a house cost $85,000. I put $15,000 down and the seller carried the balance for three years at no interest and no payments (except, of course, for the last)! You, too, can very likely find a seller who is willing to give you financing on the purchase of your lot.

TIP

The reason that lot sellers will often give you financing is that it's so hard to sell bare land. Few people can come up with the cash. Hence, the seller is obliged to carry the financing, at least for a short time, until the buyer can put up a house and get a takeout loan to pay off both the construction loan and the cost of the lot.

How do you know if the seller will carry back paper? Most sellers will come right out and say they will carry back at least half the value of the lot. You can then make them an offer of carrying back 90 percent, or whatever fits your financing needs.

TRAP

Lenders won't allow a superior mortgage on a lot ahead of their own construction loan. ("Superior" means that in the event of foreclosure, it would get paid off first before any "inferior" loans.) Hence, you have to be sure that the seller of the lot is willing to subordinate the lot loan, making it second in line in terms of who gets the money if there's a foreclosure. Some lenders are very strict and won't even allow a subordinated second on the lot. If that's the case, then you'll just have to jump to a more lenient and reasonable lender.

What Should I Look For in a Lot?

Obviously, the lot should be pleasing to you. Most people prefer larger lots. Views are considered a premium. Water frontage is a major premium. However, in addition to being in a good location, buying a lot also has a lot of pitfalls. Here are a few things to especially watch out for:

- *Drainage.* You want water to drain away from, not into, your lot. Be wary of buying a lot in the summer when everything is dry only to discover in the winter that your lot turns into a quagmire. Ask and make sure the seller signs a disclosure saying there are no drainage problems. Check with neighbors and the county planning and building departments to see if they have any negative reports on the site.

- *Utilities.* In order to build, you at least need to have power and potable water. Natural gas and TV cable are also desirable. Hopefully, these are already in place right up to the edge of the lot. If not, you have to determine how you're going to get them. Satellite can substitute for cable. Propane can substitute for natural gas. A well can bring in water. However, if you don't have electricity, then you may want to pass on the lot. Yes, there are farms out in the boonies with no electric hookup, but don't expect any lender to offer good financing on them soon.

  A developed lot will have all the utilities and these will be included in the purchase price. An undeveloped lot will not have utilities and you'll have to bring them in, something that can be extremely costly. Just bringing electricity a mile can cost tens of thousands of dollars.

- *Roads.* You have to be able to get in and out of your lot. Hopefully, there's a road there. On the other hand, if you have an undeveloped lot, you'll need to put in the roads. That could be extremely costly and make the lot off limits in terms of price.

Be sure that you've not only got roads, but the right to use them. Landlocked lots with no egress or ingress (out or in) are a well-known problem in land sales. Don't get stuck buying one.

- *Site.* Hopefully, your lot will include a site suitable for building. This is a flat piece of land on which you can construct a home. Some lots are too steep to have a site. I once was offered a 3-acre lot in a choice area for an incredibly low price. Of course, it turned out the lot was on the steep side of a hill. It would have required building on stilts to put up a house. Naturally, I refused.

- *Soil.* The ideal soil is a bit gravelly so that it will give good support to a foundation. Beware of soggy soil with a high water table that's marshlike. Also avoid soil that has lots of boulders, which can require expensive blasting to remove, or a shale band, which can be difficult to get through and which may have uncertain soil beneath.

- *Trees.* Most people love a wooded lot. Indeed, lots with mature trees on them often sell for significantly more than bare lots. However, too many trees can be a problem. It can cost upwards of $500 to cut and haul away a tree. If your lot is covered with them, it can get quite expensive to clear a building site.

TRAP

Always get a professional survey of the lot. This will tell you where the boundaries truly are. This way, you can make sure nobody else has already encroached with a building on a portion of the lot. And it will also tell you where within the lot you can put up your building.

TIP

Always walk the lot before you buy. You never know what you'll find, from a skunk hollow to half-buried garbage. It's better to know before hand and have the seller take care of it, than to buy and have the expense of dealing with the problem yourself.

What about a Sewer Hookup?

If you purchase a lot in an urban area, this should be no problem. There will undoubtedly be a public sanitary sewer in the street in front. Be aware, however, that when you hook up, you'll be charged for your share of putting in the sewer. It could be in the form of a bond over a period of 5 to 15 years and could be quite expensive. (Sometimes the bond assessment is already on the lot. If it is, try to have the seller pay it off!)

On the other hand, if you're in a rural area you may need to install a septic system. This, too, can be quite expensive. It involves creating a leach field to handle liquid waste and installing a septic tank for solid waste. The complete installation these days can cost upwards of $10,000 or more.

TRAP

Before you buy a lot requiring a septic system, be sure there's enough room for two leach fields. These take up a large area of land—sometimes as much as 30 by 30 or more depending on the soil conditions. Many building departments now require room for a second leach field in the event the first gets plugged up. It might just turn out that if there isn't enough room for the leach fields, the lot is undevelopable!

Get a Set of Building Plans

At one time this was a very expensive and difficult task. Today, it can be a breeze. There are dozens of magazines out there that are filled with home building plans. They show you several elevations of how the structure will look when finished. If you like what you see, for about $500 you can send in for a complete set of working drawings— the kind that the building department needs and builders use.

TRAP

Do not attempt to use plans from a magazine until you've had them checked by an architect and a structural engineer. You want to be sure that they will work and are safe. This can cost you an additional $500 to $1,500.

Also, if you've contacted a contractor, he or she may have a set of plans they have used before that could be used for your structure.

This has the added advantage that the contractor knows to the dollar how much the materials and labor cost to put up the house.

TRAP

Be sure your plans are "engineered." This means a structural engineer has gone through and specified the size of all lumber to be used. Also specified is where any steel must be used. A house that's not properly engineered can collapse in heavy wind or snow!

Finally, you can always hire an architect to come up with a set of original plans for you. However, this will be the most costly way to go. Architects may charge a set fee (expect to pay at least $3,500 to $5,000 for a full set of plans) or a percentage of the cost of the building (5 percent for starters). Of course, this also includes supervision of the job. In theory, a good architect can save you more than his or her cost by cutting corners and watching spending on materials and labor.

TIP

A full set of working plans includes at least three exterior elevations and interior layouts plus separate blueprints for foundation; structure; electrical, plumbing, and heating; and so on. By the way, the term blueprint referred to a method of making copies of large prints on blue paper. Today, large copying machines make prints on white paper.

What Do I Do with the Plans?

You'll need at least half a dozen sets. The lender will need a full set in order to evaluate the building and determine how much it will loan.

The building department will usually want three sets: one to keep in a central office file, one to keep at the local office to be available to anyone who wants to check it out, and one to give back to you to keep on site to be available to inspectors.

The contractor will want a set in order to come up with a bid on the amount and cost of materials and labor. And each subcontractor will need one for the same reason. (Usually the same couple of sets are transferred around between subs.)

How Do I Hire a Contractor and Subs?

This is the most delicate part of the building process. Who you hire to work for you will make all the difference in how well the job comes out and in how timely it's done. You want to hire the best you can afford. And that's sometimes tricky because you may not know anyone in the field.

My suggestion is that you start at a building supply store. Typically, there are several in the area that supply materials to contractors. Ask the people there for the names of the three top independent builders in the area. After you check with a couple of stores, one or two names will keep cropping up. Then go to see them.

Typically, they'll be very busy, but usually not too busy for a new prospect. Tell them you're going to be building your own home and see if you can work out some sort of a fee arrangement with them (assuming you don't want to hire them as full-time contractors). If you do, then have them take care of hiring the subcontractors.

If they aren't willing to do this, as they probably won't be given their busy schedules, ask them for the names of a couple of subs (such as concrete, electrical, plumbing, and so on). They'll probably give you the names of the best around. Most important, ask them if they know of a carpenter who can act as a contractor for you. Often they'll have someone in their crew or know of someone who's ready to move up. Usually they won't stand in this person's way, and they'll give you the name.

All that you actually need are a couple of names to get started. Go and see these people. If they're subs, get their commitment to work for you when it's time for their specialty. Suddenly, you're on your way.

TIP

One person leads to another. I've moved into a completely new area and found the name of one person in the building trades who was recommended as reliable. I contacted him and he led me to half a dozen more.

And those led to everyone I needed. The building
trades are a small society; everyone knows everyone.
And they also know who's good at it and who isn't. If
you team up with a good carpenter, plumber, or whatever, he or she can very quickly lead you to everyone
else you need.

Keep in mind that if you're going to be your own contractor,
you'll need to hire all of the subs. That means contacting them, giving them a set of plans so they know what's required, and getting
bids. If this sounds intimidating, it's because it's new to you. That's
the advantage of having someone, such as a carpenter or builder,
working for you who can advise and fill in the spaces when you're
out of your league.

How Do I Do the Actual Work?

The order of construction pretty much follows the chart given earlier
in this chapter for construction loan payments. It's obvious. You start
with the foundation, not the roof. We don't have room to go over
the entire construction process in this short chapter, but here's a
breakdown of what you'll be doing so you can judge whether or not
it's something you'd feel comfortable with.

Grading

Your first task will be grading and bringing utility lines to the house
itself. I've actually rented a tractor and done this myself and can tell
you it's a waste of your time. It will take you longer to learn how to
use the equipment than it will to hire someone to do it for you. Also,
because a grading contractor knows exactly what he or she is doing,
the contractor can be in and out in a day. Thus, the contractor's
costs might actually be less than the cost of renting a tractor for a
week of playing around on your own.

Be sure that the grading contractor digs the trenches for the
sewer and utility lines.

TRAP

The tendency is to put all of the lines in the same hole. Some building departments will allow this, others won't. If yours does, it will save you money. Just be sure that the sewer line is on the bottom, the water line in the middle, and the electrical line on top. That's for safety sake and also for ease of working if you ever have to dig them up.

Foundation

This is heavy work involving digging trenches, lashing together rebar (reinforcing steel bars), and pouring concrete. It's also fairly costly work.

If you've got a strong back and are up to doing heavy manual labor, then you can tackle this. But be sure that you get someone well versed in building foundations to lay it all out for you. If it's not done right, it's literally set in concrete. And if it's wrong, yours wouldn't be the first foundation that a building inspector required to be torn out and redone correctly!

If you can afford it, I strongly suggest you hire this out to a contractor. He or she can be in and out in a few days, and you'll have a good foundation on which to build your house.

TRAP

Be sure that all of the utility and sewer lines lead through the foundation and that all of the "J" bolts (used to bolt down the house) are placed in the cement while it's wet. Otherwise, either the foundation will have to be redone or holes drilled in and through it, thus weakening it.

The building department will take samples of the concrete used in the foundation in what look like one pound coffee cans. Hydraulic jacks will compress the concrete 7 days, 14 days, and 28 days after the sample is taken. If the concrete does not meet minimum standards for strength, it will have to be torn out and a new foundation laid. Another reason to be sure it's done right the first time.

TIP

The person laying the foundation and calling for the concrete will determine what plasticizers and other chemicals are added to it. These can extend the time that the cement is liquid, but can also weaken it. You want the strongest concrete possible.

Framing

This goes up pretty fast, and it's an area where you can participate. Just two people, you and a carpenter, can frame an entire house in a couple of weeks.

Be aware, however, that it involves lifting heavy timbers. It's not the sort of thing for bad backs or hernias. You won't save a lot of money doing it yourself, but you'll save some. And you'll have the satisfaction of seeing your own home built from the ground up.

Roof

You can have a roofer put this on. It can be done in a couple of days. Or you can do it yourself.

The roof base is usually some form of plywood. This is laid over the rafters and nailed down. It's not a difficult job and much like putting together a jigsaw puzzle.

If you're doing a fiberglass, asphalt, or wood shingle roof, it's fairly easy to do. The materials are heavy, but you can have them delivered right to the roof! Then it's just a matter of following the pattern and nailing them down. So what if it takes you a couple of weeks? Assuming it's summer, and not raining or snowing, it can be very enjoyable working out in the sun. (Wear sunscreen!)

On the other hand, if the roof is tile of any sort, it's best left to experts. Tile requires that an underlayment be placed down, which actually keeps the water out. This underlayment must be kept intact while walking on it and putting down the tiles. All of this is quite tricky and best left to experts.

TRAP

Tile roofs will last almost indefinitely. But that's after they're put up. Walking on them, even just once, can result in lots of broken tile. If you're trying to do this yourself and it's your first time, chances are you'll break more in tile than it will cost you to have a contractor do the entire job!

Rough Electrical, Plumbing, and Heating

This is where you can save big bucks. Electrical and plumbing work is usually the most costly. Yet, it is all logical. If you can find a professional to work with you showing you how, and if you can learn the basics from a book, you may be able to do it all yourself and save loads of money.

WARNING! Do *not* attempt to do any electrical work with the power on. Do *not* do any work involving electricity, gas, or plumbing unless you are qualified to do so.

TIP

In many states, electrical, gas, and plumbing work can only be done by licensed contractors. However, in most states, if you agree to personally live in the home for a period of time, typically six months to a year, you can get a permit to do the work yourself. If you do the work yourself, be sure you get it thoroughly inspected and approved by a professional.

Skin

Putting the exterior on the house is done after the framing is completed and about the same time as the roof is going on and the rough utilities are done.

The skin can be composed of anything from wood sheathing to shingles to stone. It just must be composed of a surface that's impenetrable to moisture.

It's common practice these days to wrap the house in a sealing material, such as fiberglass paper, before putting on the outer skin. This helps with insulation and moisture control.

Be aware that if you use natural wood as an exterior, it will require constant maintenance in the form of staining or painting. Left without coating, it can crack and deteriorate in only a few years.

Again, you can do all of this work yourself. With sheathing, it's mostly a matter of cutting and fitting pieces in place. With siding, it's a matter of getting the lines straight. Each surface has its own requirements and difficulties, but first timers can usually master them.

Windows are put in at this time. You'll want to use double-pane windows to save money later on heating and cooling. Use of low-E coatings, which reduce the transmission of radiant heat, are big money savers in the long run. With a little instruction, there's no reason you can't install windows and doors yourself.

Insulate

Today, all homes are insulated as an energy conserving measure. The insulation is measured by its "R" factor, which tells how well it insulates. The higher the R factor is, the greater the insulation.

Your local building department will tell you the minimum R factor you can use for ceilings, walls, and floors. It will also tell you the type of insulation to use—whether rolled, rigid, blown, or some other.

You won't save any money by doing this yourself. But you will get fiberglass cuts all over your body, and chances are you'll inhale enough of the stuff to be coughing for weeks.

The cost of having a professional do it is often about the same as for you to buy the fiberglass at a building materials store and do it yourself. The reason is that installers get huge discounts. And they are incredibly quick, often able to insulate an entire house in a single day.

Drywall, Tape, and Texture

Assuming you're going to use Sheetrock inside, you can do all this work yourself. Drywall is hard to work with only because it's very heavy. But it's not complicated to get it cut and into place. Just have someone show you how it's done.

Taping is what's done to the edges of two pieces of drywall. Paper tape coated in drywall paste is laid over them making a finished seal. There are machines available today that make this an extremely easy process. Typically you'll need to sand and then plaster the taped area several times to get a perfectly smooth finish.

Finally, the whole thing is textured. This typically produces an orange peel effect with many shadows so that the taping becomes invisible. Typically it's done using a "cannon" that blows it onto the walls. The text may then be troweled, or not, depending on the look you want.

Putting up drywall, taping, and texturing is not expensive. The cost is typically only a few thousand dollars. Yes, you can save money doing it yourself. But chances are you'll get a far better job at minimal cost by hiring it out. And remember, this shows.

Finish Plumbing, Electrical, and Heating

This involves going around putting in the plugs and sockets, attaching the electrical and plumbing fixtures, and so on. Check the warnings noted above for roughing. They also apply here.

If you're qualified to do it, you can save a bundle of money. As noted, these are the most expensive of the building trades. And they don't take long. You should be able to rough in the various items in only a few days, depending on the size of the house.

Finish Carpentry and Floors

This involves putting on all the moldings around windows and doors. It also involves putting in the flooring.

The moldings are something that most people who are handy with wood not only can do, but enjoy doing. Get yourself a good chop saw and you'll have a ball doing it.

The flooring, on the other hand, might be best left to pros. Certainly, if you're opting for wall-to-wall carpeting, you'll want the pros to lay it. It only takes them a day for an entire house. The same holds for linoleum.

On the other hand, if it's wood flooring, you may want to do it yourself. Just be prepared for painstaking work that may last over several weeks, depending on how fast you go.

Pergo and other synthetic wood floors are faster, but require specific tools, glues, and skills. Get trained in the laying of these before attempting them.

Tile is something that you can do. Since you do it one piece (or one square of one foot by one foot tiles) at a time, you can go as fast or as slow as you need. Just be sure that you bone up on how it's done. Many supply stores, such as Home Depot, offer courses in tile laying.

If you do it yourself, with the exception of carpeting and linoleum, you can save big bucks. Just remember, however, it means you'll be on your hands and knees for long periods of time.

Appliances and Fixtures

If you've done the plumbing and electrical yourself, you'll certainly want to install these items yourself. Sinks are the most difficult because you have to get in and under them. Tubs and showers are the heaviest.

Most stoves and ovens simply plug in and out.

Painting

If you have the time, certainly you can do this yourself. Figure $5,000 to hire someone to paint the house inside and out. For under $1,000, you can buy all the paint, drop cloths, rollers, brushes, and other supplies and do it yourself.

Finish the Financing

As you go through the building process, you'll constantly be having inspections. The building department will be there all the time (or at least it will seem that way). And your lender will also likely have someone come by to check out how you're coming.

Eventually, though, you'll get "finaled" by the building department and then you'll get your final payment from the lender. Now all that's left is to go back to the lender (or a different one, if you choose) and get that big permanent takeout loan that will pay off the construction loan and, hopefully, most of the cost of the lot.

Now you've got your affordable home, and not just a little pride to go with it.

TRAP

Beware of "mechanic's liens." Any supplier of labor or materials can put this lien on your property if you fail to pay them. Problems can occur if a contractor is supposed to pay the subs, but doesn't. In that case, the subs can legally come after you for payment, even if you've already paid the contractor! Be sure you understand how mechanic's liens work and take steps to avoid them.

For much more information on mechanic's liens and on constructing your own home, check out my book *Tips & Traps When Building Your Home* (McGraw-Hill, 2000).

BUILDING A HOME QUIZ

	YES	NO
1. You can save 30 percent or more by building yourself?	[ ]	[ ]
2. Building departments will not let you do the work?	[ ]	[ ]
3. Your first step should be arranging the financing?	[ ]	[ ]
4. A construction loan offers you many small payments?	[ ]	[ ]
5. A "takeout" loan is permanent financing?	[ ]	[ ]
6. Lenders don't require expert supervision of construction?	[ ]	[ ]
7. You should always have a lot surveyed?	[ ]	[ ]
8. View and wooded lots usually cost more?	[ ]	[ ]
9. A developed lot will still not have utilities?	[ ]	[ ]
10. Sewer hookup can be costly?	[ ]	[ ]
11. A septic tank may require two leach fields?	[ ]	[ ]
12. You only need one set of building plans?	[ ]	[ ]
13. You can hire your own subcontractors?	[ ]	[ ]

	YES	NO
14. Grading is easy, so do it yourself?	[ ]	[ ]
15. You'll never be asked to dig up a foundation?	[ ]	[ ]
16. You and a carpenter can do all the framing in a few weeks?	[ ]	[ ]
17. Don't plan on doing the roof if it's tile?	[ ]	[ ]
18. Insulation installation is very costly to hire out?	[ ]	[ ]
19. You can save lots of money by painting it yourself?	[ ]	[ ]
20. The permanent loan can pay off the construction and the lot?	[ ]	[ ]

ANSWERS

1. Yes	6. No	11. Yes	16. Yes
2. No	7. Yes	12. No	17. Yes
3. Yes	8. Yes	13. Yes	18. No
4. Yes	9. No	14. No	19. Yes
5. Yes	10. Yes	15. No	20. Yes

SCORE

15–20 You're a natural builder!

10–14 Be sure you hire a carpenter/contractor to help.

5–9   You may want to take a course in construction.

0–4   Buy already built!

9

How to Afford a
Home When You
Have Credit
Problems

There are many affordable mortgages out there, some for all or even more than the purchase price of a home you may be considering. However, what all of these low- or nothing-down financing plans have in common is that they require you to have good credit.

But what if you don't have such good credit? What if you've been in a situation where you've had a few late payments? Or maybe you've defaulted on a loan? Or you've had a bankruptcy? Or what's considered the most heinous of all credit problems, you've had a foreclosure!

Can you still afford to buy a home?

In this chapter, we'll look at how credit problems can affect your ability to get real estate financing. Then we'll look at ways to get around these roadblocks.

Why Good Credit Is
Important

Look at it from the lender's perspective. The lender is offering you hundreds of thousands of dollars toward the purchase of a home. This is probably the biggest financing deal that most Americans ever make. And what does the lender want in return? The lender wants to know that you'll repay the debt, with interest.

If the lender can be perfectly assured you'll repay as agreed, you'll quickly get the financing. If the lender has some doubts, then there may be some delays and the lender could ask for a higher interest rate to offset a higher risk. But if the lender believes that there's a serious chance you won't repay, you simply won't get your mortgage.

TRAP

Many people are surprised to learn that even a few late payments can seriously affect their ability to get real estate financing. The attitude "I'll pay when I'm good and ready" may sound defiant against a creditor whom you dislike. But when those late payments show up on your credit report, your future mortgage lender wonders if you'll say the same thing to it?

How Does the Lender Know If You'll Repay?

When you apply for a mortgage, you'll be asked to fill out a standard loan application. It has about 60 questions on it that cover whole categories of your personal finances including the following:

- Your income
- Your expenses
- The amount of cash you're putting down
- Your reserves (money in the bank)
- Your long-term debt
- And more

The lender will look at what you put down and attempt to see whether you have enough income to qualify for a mortgage. The lender will also be very interested in your credit history.

As part of that application you'll also give identifying information such as a your full name(s), past addresses, and social security number. Based on this information, the lender will run a three-bureau credit check (sometimes called a "standard factual").

There are three national credit bureaus, Experion, Transunion, and Equifax. They contain input from many other smaller credit-reporting agencies around the country. If you've paid your bills on time, that will show up on this report. And if you haven't paid bills on time and have other problems, that will show up as well.

It might seem a simple matter to take a look at a credit report and say, "This person has good credit—we'll give him a mortgage." Or, "That person has bad credit—we'll deny him a mortgage."

However, it's not that easy. While it's only common sense that whether you paid in the past is a likely indicator of whether you will pay in the future, exactly how does your earlier credit performance indicate future behavior? How does a lender know with any certainty what you'll do? Maybe you were out of work and had credit problems, but now you've got a solid job and will perform as agreed. Maybe you were going through a divorce or an illness. Now you're more stable.

A credit report is only figures on a piece of paper. How does the lender evaluate it?

The answer is that lenders rely, in part, on special companies to do that evaluation for them. The biggest of these is FICO (Fair Isaac) in California. FICO analyzes your credit report and then gives you a score between 300 and 900. The higher your score, the better a borrower you are and the more likely you'll get a mortgage. The lower your rating, the more likely you'll be late on payments or default on your loan, and the less likely you are to get financing.

If you've applied for a mortgage recently, chances are you have a FICO score and you can learn what it is. Simply go to *www.fairisaac.com* online. (You can also obtain it through *www.experion.com*.) You'll get your score for a fee. The FICO site also provides all sorts of information on how your FICO score is determined and gives a few clues on how to raise it.

Who Are the Lenders Who Evaluate Your Score?

We've been glossing over this, but presumably we're talking about the company that will actually offer you the mortgage, right? It's the company that looks at your FICO score and determines whether or not to extend financing, right?

Wrong! As it turns out in today's real estate mortgage market, the company whose name appears on the mortgage documents you get is usually nothing more than a servicer. It originates the loan and then collects payments from you. The actual money usually comes from one of two sources, Fannie Mae or Freddie Mac (which are called secondary lenders). These are huge quasi-government corporations that loan billions of dollars on real estate. They are the ones who give thumbs up or thumbs down on your mortgage. Here's how it works.

You apply for a mortgage through Al, a mortgage broker. He sends your application to XYZ mortgage company. XYZ forwards your application, for example, to Fannie Mae's underwriting department. The underwriters look at your application and your FICO score and then apply a profile of their own. Depending on how it all comes out, Fannie Mae tells XYZ whether you'll get the loan and what kind you'll get. XYZ then passes the information on to your mortgage broker who lets you know. That's the overall process.

Profiling? Did Someone Say Profiling?

We're talking financial profiling here (although most lenders don't like to use that term). The underwriters have a database of hundreds of thousands of successful and unsuccessful borrowers. From that database they create profiles of what successful mortgage applicants will look like. They then try to fit you into one of these profiles.

TIP

The profiles I've seen can be quite extraordinary. For example, if someone puts 30 percent down on a property, but has no credit, they may still qualify for a mortgage simply because past history shows people with this much to put down almost never default. They have a successful profile. Another borrower who has meticulously made payments for 20 years may need nothing down. Past history may reveal that this sort of profile also almost never defaults. On the other hand, someone who has applied for credit a half dozen times in the months before applying for the mortgage may be turned down completely. Past history may suggest a person with this profile is a bad risk.

Thus, the underwriters have your credit report, your credit score, and their own profiles based on past financial history to determine how you'll fare. Even so, they rarely give a simple pass or fail. Rather, you'll end up with a letter grade, typically from A to D.

Mortgage lenders see borrowers in a range between those who they are positive will repay, whom they call "prime," and those who they are worried will not repay, called "subprime." Prime borrowers have no credit problems, strong income, and lots of cash in the bank. They are also the "A" borrowers. Everyone else is subprime and is rated from "A–" down to "D."

See "Borrowers from A to D" that follows for a brief description of how a letter rating system can work. Keep in mind this applies to no particular lender, but rather is a composite. Each lender has its own yardstick.

You can be an excellent credit risk, yet by doing something as simple as carrying high balances on a couple of credit cards you might lower your rating. On the other hand, you may be a terrible credit risk, but by presenting your credit information in just the right light you can secure surprisingly good financing.

Can Every Category Get Financing?

Yes and no. Obviously, if you're a prime "A" borrower, the best loans are available to you.

However, if you're in a lesser category then, in theory, other types of financing are available to you as well. A few years back it was simply a matter of increasing the interest rate. Prime borrowers got the market rate. Subprime had to contend with a higher rate. For example, if you were a "D" borrower your LTV might be lower and you might have to pay as much as 5 percent more on your mortgage.

Severe default rates by subprime borrowers over the last few years, however, have derailed many of the programs that catered to them.

Borrowers from A to D	
Rating	Description
A	Most creditworthy.
A–	One unpaid bill, under $1,000, turned into collection or no more than one late payment of over 60 days or two late payments of over 30 days in credit cards or installment debt within the past 2 years. No bankruptcies or foreclosures on record (at least the previous 7 years).
B	Within the past 1½ years, you have up to four late payments of no more than 30 days for credit cards or installment debt. You may have had a bankruptcy or a foreclosure concluded at least 2 years before applying for loan.
C	Within the past year you have up to six late payments of no more than 30 days on credit cards or installment debt. You may have accounts currently in collection, but the mortgage may be granted if they are no more than $5,000 and paid in full by the time the mortgage is funded. Mortgage funds may be used to clean up these debts. If you have a bankruptcy, it was resolved at least a year before applying for the mortgage. If you had a foreclosure, it was concluded at least 2 years before applying for the loan.
D	You have many current late payments, have several accounts in collection, and have judgments against you. These can be paid off from the proceeds of the new mortgage. If you have a bankruptcy, it was concluded more than 6 months before you applied for the new mortgage. If you had a foreclosure, it was concluded at least 2 years before applying for the loan.

Today, if you're severely subprime you might have trouble finding a mortgage. Check with your mortgage broker to see what's available at the time you're looking.

Can You Improve Your Credit Rating?

That's the $64,000 question. Most scoring companies suggest that it's possible to improve your score in only a modest way. For example, FICO has pointed out that applying for credit too many times (more than three, for example) within months of applying for your mortgage could lower your score. Thus, the suggestion is not to apply for credit unless and until you actually need it.

TIP

Simply checking on your credit by buying a credit report directly from a credit bureau should not count as applying for credit. For this reason, most financial advisers suggest you check on your credit report once or twice a year just to be sure there are no errors.

I've been observing the mortgage industry and how credit scoring and credit categories are built and the following are my own observations. There's no guarantee that doing any of the following will improve your standing. On the other hand, it shouldn't hurt.

Your Income versus Expenses

Your income is obviously how much money you make before taxes. It includes such things as alimony. If both spouses have a long history of career work, their entire salaries may be counted. On the other hand, if one spouse works only part-time or has only a short work history, only a portion of his or her income may be counted. Your expenses include PITI (principal, interest, taxes, and insurance) on the property plus living expenses plus other debt.

When filling out a mortgage application, it usually pays to emphasize length and continuity. For example, you're a teacher who has gotten his first job in years just a month ago. The lender is bound to wonder if you will succeed at the work. However, if you note that you were a teacher with 5 years experience a decade ago before leaving the field to help raise children, it can help put your application in a whole new and better light.

Are You Self-Employed?

The method by which you receive your income is important too. If you work for an employer and receive wages (meaning a W-2 form at the end of the year), you get preference mainly because it is easy to verify your income and because you presumably have something called "job security." (The only way a lender can determine this is by asking your employer what your chances for future employment are—a question frequently asked!)

On the other hand, if you're self-employed you may be turned down without further consideration. Sometimes prime loans simply will not be granted to self-employed individuals. In other cases you will be asked to produce the last 2 years of your 1040 federal tax filings. The concern here is actually verifying your income because you could submit false records. (Today, many lenders are capable of verifying income directly with the IRS!) And when you are self-employed, unless you can show a long work history, you are presumed to be at risk of job loss.

Thus, if you can show income as an employee, you're usually far better off than if you can only show income as a self-employed person.

What's the Size of Your Income?

The amount of your income will have to be big enough to allow you to make the mortgage payments plus have sufficient money left over for all your living expenses plus taxes. Complex formulas for "front end" (the ratio of your house payment including principal, interest, taxes, and insurance to your income) as compared with "back end" (the ratio of your total expense payments to your gross income) are used.

Suffice to say you need as much income as possible. Thus, if possible, it is usually a good idea to pay off any short-term debt (such as credit cards) *before* applying for a mortgage. That way you increase your income (less is set aside to pay for the short-term debt) and you may have a better chance of qualifying. On the other hand, the more of your available cash you use to pay off debt, the less you will have available for a down payment and closing costs. Again, it's a trade-off.

How Much Cash Are You Putting Down?

You usually want to put as little as possible down. From the lender's perspective, however, the more you put down the better. The reason is the more you have into the property of your own money, the less likely you are to let it go to foreclosure if the market turns down or you lose your job. The more you have in, presumably, the harder you'll fight to keep the home.

If you want to better your likelihood of getting financing, try to put more cash down.

Another consideration is where you get the money for the down payment. Ideally it will be your own money earned over the years and set aside as savings. Borrowing the down payment can be a problem. Borrowing the down payment suggests to the underwriter that you really can't afford the property. Let the lender know you're borrowing your down payment and you could be scuttling the loan.

Therefore, if you need to borrow money that you intend to use as part of the down payment, do it well in advance of applying for the mortgage (at least 6 months). That way the money will be seen as part of a savings account and the loan will be long established. In other words, you won't be borrowing specifically to make the home purchase.

Gifts for the down payment from relatives are usually acceptable. These must, however, be legitimate gifts. They can't be given with strings attached, such as you'll repay them so much a month and when you sell the property you'll repay the balance in full. In that case, they are nothing more than a disguised loan.

In the past, many underwriters insisted that those offering gifts as part of the down payment and closing costs co-sign the mortgage and also qualify for it. This effectively nixed the deal in many cases. That requirement, however, has recently been removed for many federally underwritten mortgages. Today, a gift with a simple gift letter may suffice. Check with your lender.

How Big Are Your Cash Reserves?

Reserves are what you have left in the bank after you make the down payment and take care of the closing costs. Ideally, lenders would like to see at least 1 month or more worth of monthly expenses. If you don't have any money in reserve, you could be turned down or more likely be asked to accept a smaller mortgage.

You can usually improve your credit standing by withholding at least a month's worth of cash in the bank. Not easily done, but something to consider.

Have You Repaid Your Past Debts?

The credit companies check the public records to see if you have had any bankruptcies or foreclosures. They also look for any loans you have that are now in collection.

The credit agencies also try to determine whether you are delinquent in any of your trade lines (credit cards). Any adverse notation can be cause for not issuing the mortgage.

Therefore, if you're behind in payments, catch up *before* applying for the mortgage. Try to stay caught up for at least a year before applying so your delinquencies will show up as old rather than recent. Old delinquencies are much easier to forgive.

However, be aware that frequent and severe delinquent payments can also sink you, even if you're caught up now. The best policy is to preserve your good credit by always paying on time. If you can make the payments, don't borrow the money.

A recent bankruptcy can sink you. However, if it's been more than 2 years, the lender may simply ignore it. (Bankruptcies are carried on your credit report often for a minimum of 7 years and sometimes much longer.) A foreclosure listed on your credit, however, is almost never ignored. Lenders don't like to offer mortgages to people who have in the past allowed their homes to sink into foreclosure. However, in some special cases (see the next chapter) if the foreclosure is more than 3 years old it may be ignored.

How Much Do You Owe?

What are the recent balances on all of your trade lines and the average balances over the past 6 months? How close are you to your credit limits?

The underwriters are concerned about people who live on their credit. They don't mind if you borrow as long as you have plenty of credit left. On the other hand, if you have 10 credit cards and are borrowed to the limit on all of them, it suggests a poor money manager and someone who might not be able to make mortgage payments.

Therefore, if you are borrowed out before applying for a mortgage, consider paying down or at least consolidating some of your outstanding debt. Perhaps you can obtain a single loan that will not only pay off all existing debt, but leave you a considerable buffer of unused credit on your cards. It will certainly look better to your mortgage underwriter. But do it well in advance (at least 6 months) of your mortgage application. (Keeping your credit borrowing under 50 percent of your maximum credit limit is a good idea.)

How Old Are Your Credit Lines?

Lenders want to know that you've been successfully borrowing for a long time. That tells them that you're a good money manager. To determine this, they look at your oldest trade lines. The older the better.

TIP

I've had credit cards for over 20 years. When I recently applied for credit, it was noted that I didn't have long-term cards. Long term meant 30 years or more! Hang onto your old credit cards. Keep a credit card that you've had for years, even if a new credit company offers you a somewhat better deal. That old credit card shows that you have a long history and may help you get your mortgage. This is the case even if you just keep the card in a box and almost never use it!

How Much New Credit Have You Applied For?

Generally speaking, more than three credit applications in 6 months is likely a mark against you. Yes, it's irrational, but go argue with a profile.

Similarly, if you open too many new credit card or other charge accounts, it looks suspiciously like you may be planning to borrow a lot of money and leave the country. The underwriters check your most recent new accounts. An account opened in the previous 3 months is not good.

What Is Your Credit Mix?

A good balance between credit cards, car loans, personal finance companies, and other installment loans is best. You don't want a lot of any of these or even a huge total. But the fact that you've got a car loan, three credit cards (the ideal number!), and perhaps a department store card and you've maintained reasonable balances all suggests you're a good credit manager. And that's what the underwriters actually want the most.

Can I Be Approved for a Mortgage If I Agree to Changes?

Chances are that if you have reasonably good credit, you won't be turned down for a new mortgage. Rather, if you're not approved outright, you'll be given a conditional approval provided that certain conditions are fulfilled.

These conditions may be something as simple as providing missing documentation, such as a W-2 form or an old paycheck stub. Or they might be something more severe. The underwriter may feel that in order for you to meet their standards you must increase your down payment and, accordingly, reduce the amount you are borrowing. (That's a lot to ask. You may not have any more cash and may need the maximum loan. If that's the case, the answer could be "sorry.") In some cases, you may be asked to take a course on money management.

Can I Have Bad Credit Fixed?

That depends on what the trouble is. It's a mistaken belief that you can have *all* bad credit "fixed." Companies that offer to fix or make *any* credit problem simply disappear, particularly if they charge you a hefty fee for doing it, may be nothing more than scams.

On the other hand, there are many credit fixers out there today who can improve your credit. These are companies, however, that do for you (for a fee) what you can do for yourself.

For example, if your credit is bad for the following reasons, it probably can be fixed.

Bad Credit That Can Be Fixed

- The wrong name is on the report.
- The wrong address is on the report.
- Someone else's social security number is on your report.
- A creditor made a mistake in reporting a late payment.
- A creditor has not removed a loan that's on your name, even though it's been paid off.
- You redeemed your property, yet it shows up as a foreclosure.
- You did not file for bankruptcy, yet one shows up against you.

You get the idea. Mistakes and errors can be corrected. But it takes time and effort to do so.

TIP

You can do it yourself. For example, I moved a few years ago and forwarded my new address to all of my creditors. However, one bank lost my forwarded address. I had a credit card from them, but hadn't used that card for 6 months. Then I charged a hundred dollars or so on it. They sent the bill to my old address and the post office didn't forward it. Ultimately they sent my name to a credit-reporting agency for slow payment. A few months later I finally got a copy of the bill, called the credit card company, explained the problem, and paid my bill. But the slow pay designation remained on my credit report until I discovered it there when applying for a mortgage. I then went back to the credit card company and explained the reason I had not paid was that they had not properly registered my new address. When I got the bill, I paid it promptly. They checked their records and discovered I was correct. They then issued a correction to the credit-reporting bureau and a letter to me confirming that. Time elapsed in correcting the problem was 5 months!

Credit fixers, for a fee, will go through all the hassle of correcting the mistakes and errors. Their fees are not small, but given the difficulties in correcting these sorts of problems it may well be worth it!

On the other hand, if you have credit that is truly bad, it cannot be fixed.

Bad Credit That Cannot Be Fixed

- Late payments (without a reason)
- Missed payments (without a reason)
- Loan defaults
- Bankruptcies
- Foreclosures

The best advice is to simply pay all your bills on time. Nothing messes up your credit quicker than late payments. Yet, these often result from carelessness or forgetfulness. Keep all bills in a special spot and make it a point to pay them at least once a week. This is probably the simplest, yet most effective, step you can take toward preserving your good credit.

TIP

If you find that you're unable to pay all of your bills, at least make your mortgage payment. If there's only one bill that you can pay, be sure it's your mortgage. Foreclosure and late mortgage payments are the one thing that mortgage lenders are very reluctant to forgive.

What If I'm Having an Argument with a Creditor?

What if you feel a bill is unjustified, yet the creditor insists that you pay it or be turned in to a credit-reporting agency?

Don't panic. Each state and the federal government have procedures that must be followed when a creditor pursues you. If they don't follow these, they can be in hot water with big fines. Check with an attorney, your state's consumer agency, or with the Federal Trade Commission.

TRAP

If you're concerned that a creditor may turn you into a credit-reporting agency over a disputed bill, one way to avoid this problem is to pay the creditor in full. Then sue them in small claims court for the amount. You often stand an excellent chance in small claims court of recouping your money, and since this requires the creditor to spend time in court, plus perhaps give back the money, it teaches them a real lesson.

What Sorts of Explanations Will Lender's Accept?

Lenders are human, too, and they realize that sometimes creditworthy people get into trouble. If your explanation shows that you at least tried to solve the problem and, perhaps even more important, that the problem was isolated and isn't likely to happen again, you may very well be able to get the financing you want—even a prime mortgage!

The best way to do this is to be up front with the lender. Don't wait for the problem to surface as part of your credit report. Get it out front. And provide the lender with a clearly written letter of explanation. If you have late payments, explain why they were late. If you defaulted on a loan, give all the details and include verifying information. If you had a foreclosure, explain how it occurred and why circumstances are different now.

Explanations a Lender Might Accept

You Were Unemployed or Sick. This may be acceptable if you have a long history of excellent credit broken by a short period, say 6 months, of poor credit, followed by another long period (at least 2 years) of good credit. This explanation is particularly helpful in explaining late payments.

You Had a Divorce or Death in the Family. Here again, you normally must show that this happened some time ago and since that time you've had excellent credit. This is particularly useful when you've defaulted on loans. You had a big setback in your life, but now you're back in the saddle as evidenced by at least 2 years' worth of good credit history.

Someone Else Made Me Do It. A lame excuse, but sometimes it's the truth. Perhaps you co-signed for someone else on a car. They ran off with the car and never made the payments. You were stuck with either making payments for 5 years on a car you didn't have and couldn't sell, or simply refusing. You refused.

This shows you had the good sense to not get in debt over your head. However, it also shows that you had the bad sense to co-sign for someone else. Further, given tough circumstances, instead of plodding on and making payments you'll bail out—something that makes good sense to you, but which lenders don't particularly like to see.

You Got In over Your Head. You live in California and bought during the dot-com craze. You couldn't sell or rent the property, and you had to move to Florida to keep your job. You weren't there to take care of your property and, consequently, you lost it to foreclosure.

But that was a couple of years ago, and it was on rental real estate. Here and now you're trying to buy a home in which you plan to live. The circumstances are different. Maybe the lender will agree.

It Was a Natural Disaster. There was a tornado that destroyed not only your home, but also the factory where you work. You had no place to live and no way to earn income. Naturally, you had to let your house go into foreclosure. But since then the factory is rebuilt, and you're back at work. You're ready to start again buying a house.

What about Mistakes Made by the Credit Bureau?

As many as a third of all credit reports contain an error of some kind. Even if the error is the fault of the credit bureau, it can still cause you to be declined for a mortgage. When that happens, you need to get out and correct that error. (This is another good reason to order your own credit report early on. You can discover if there are errors and take steps to correct them.)

Generally speaking, the best approach to take in correcting errors is to obtain proof that it is indeed an error. Then write to the credit-reporting agency offering the proof and demand the error be corrected. The credit agency must investigate your request and take action within a month or two.

The trick is getting the proof. What's usually accepted is a letter or document from the lender reporting the bad credit and saying it was a mistake. Or, in the case of mistaken identity, it's a matter of presenting irrefutable evidence that you are who you are and not the other person the credit company thinks you are. Birth certificate, driver's license, escrow company ID statements, and so forth can help here.

Remember, the basic method of correcting bad credit is twofold. First, you have to write a letter explaining the problem and why it's the creditor's fault or an error in reporting by the credit bureau. Second, you have to submit documentation proving what you say.

How Soon Will the Credit Bureau Correct the Mistake?

That depends on your proof. If the original creditor who reported the problem now reports an error, the agency will normally remove the offending report within 30 days.

On the other hand, if your proof tends to be your word against the lender who refuses to admit an error, it's a different story. The credit-reporting agency is generally required to insert your letters of explanation along with the bad report and may make your substantiating documentation available to those who ask for reports.

The credit agency, however, doesn't usually take sides. In a disputed case, they probably will not remove the offending incident. It will stay on your report usually for up to 7 years.

For more information on how to correct an error in your credit report write to:

Federal Trade Commission
CRC-240
Washington, DC 20580
1-877-FTC-HELP (382-4357)

How Do I Get a Copy of My Credit Report?

It's a good idea to get a copy of your own credit report in advance of applying for a mortgage. That way you get to see what the lender will see and to prepare for it. You are allowed to obtain at least one copy of your credit report each year. You probably will want to get it from one of the big credit-reporting agencies. The cost is minimal.

Transunion
800-888-4213
www.tuc.com

Experian (formerly TRW)
888-397-3742
www.experian.com

Equifax
800 685.1111
www.equifax.com

What If I Have No Credit?

Having no credit is almost as bad as having terrible credit. In order to give you a mortgage, a lender has to establish your money management patterns. It does that by seeing how successfully you've paid back money that you've previously borrowed. But if you've never borrowed the lender can't establish a pattern. And in the world of borrower profiles (explained earlier in this chapter) that can leave you out in the cold.

That doesn't mean, however, that you can't otherwise establish your credit and get a mortgage. Indeed, having no credit is just an inconvenience. If you make the proper efforts, you can establish a good credit record and be years ahead of the individual who starts off with lots of bad reports.

Is It Hard to Establish Credit?

No. But begin at least 6 months, but preferably a year or more, before you plan on applying for a mortgage. It will take time to establish a good credit history. It can't be done over night.

The first thing you should do is to go to the bank where you do business (not having credit doesn't mean that you don't have a checking and savings account) and apply for a debit card. As you probably know, this is like a credit card, only based on your assets in the bank. Many banks now offer these virtually automatically to their customers.

Once you have the debit card use it frequently, establishing that you can manage such an item. Also, be scrupulous to see that you never bounce your own checks and can always cover any checks from others that you deposit. Ask your bank to establish a small line of credit to cover your checking account just in case you should be short. This overdraft credit line is also often done automatically by the bank for good, long-standing customers.

Once you have an overdraft account and a debit account, ask your bank for a credit card. Almost all banks offer them. With your good standing in the bank, it should again be automatic.

Once you get the credit card, you're halfway home. Go out and charge to the limit. Then pay it back promptly. Pay off all your charges each month for 3 months and you've established a great credit history.

Very shortly, other credit card offers should start appearing in the mail. Apply for two others. Charge a few things on these and make regular monthly payments.

Now go back to your bank and ask for a noncollateral loan—a line of credit. Say you want to buy furniture or a used car. You have your history at the bank, plus your new credit cards, plus the fact that you have no bad credit. Again, it's a slam dunk.

Borrow a thousand dollars or so this way, put it in the bank, make regular payments on it, and after a few months pay it back.

Voila! With the exception of longevity, you have just established the rudiments of prime credit. Age means how long you've had your trade lines. That first credit card you got—keep it. It will age and once it's 2 years old, you've satisfied the basic age portion.

TIP

You don't want to just establish credit. You want to establish good credit. Make all of your payments on time. If you're late or miss a payment, you'll establish credit all right, but it will be bad!

What Do I Do If I Need to Get a Mortgage Right Now and Don't Have Credit?

The above plan is great *if* you've got the time to spend. But what if you want to get a mortgage right now. You don't have time to set up credit cards and installment loans. You want to buy a home, and you have to go with what you've got. But you have an empty credit history.

Actually, almost no one's credit history is truly empty. At worst, it's usually just a case of not having thought of what to fill it with. Here are some suggestions for creating an instant credit history:

- *Rent receipts.* You must have lived somewhere and if you didn't own, you rented. If you paid rent by check, get those canceled checks. They should show a steady pattern of regular payments. Better still, get letters from your current and previous landlords stating that you made your rent payments on time. Also have the landlords state the amount to establish that you can handle a large monthly payment.

- *Utility Receipts.* You had to have electricity, water, garbage, gas, phone, and probably cable TV. You paid for these. Again look for canceled checks. Also, call up the companies and ask them for letters of recommendation. Many utility companies will do this almost automatically if you've had a good payment history for 1 year.

- Informal Loans. People who pay by cash often get loans from friends and family. If you paid these back on time, get your canceled checks or other receipts. Have the person sign a statement showing the amount borrowed, the term, when regular payments were made, and when it was paid back. If the person you borrowed from is able to put a corporate or business name on the statement, it's even better.

You might need to dig into your memory for some other account that similarly can be used to help establish your credit. Dig as deeply as possible. While none of these individually is as good as a long history of credit cards with prompt repayment, they can go a long way.

What about Getting Someone to Co-sign?

Yes, you may be able to. Some lenders will accept cosigners, some will not. If you don't have the credit history, find someone who does and make them a partner, and find a lender who will cooperate.

Relatives are usually opportune choices. Good friends, even business associates, are also likely candidates. Remember, you don't need the cosigner to help you with the down payment or the monthly payments. You just need her good, established credit.

Keep in mind, however, that when someone co-signs with you, her credit is on the line. If you default, or worse, if you lose the property to foreclosure, it will reflect badly on her credit. It will be as if she were late on payments or lost the property. For this reason, keep in mind that most savvy people will refuse to co-sign for anyone, even close relatives.

To induce another person to co-sign for you, you may want to give them an ownership position in the property. You may want her to have her name appear both on the deed and on the mortgage. That way, should you for some reason stop making payments or go into foreclosure, she could step in and take over and possibly save the property. This can be a strong inducement to a reluctant cosigner.

Most lenders will want the cosigner on the mortgage in any event. So it's just a simple step more to include her on the deed.

However, once the cosigner is on the deed, she can tie up the property and potentially keep you from selling. To protect your interests, you will want to have an attorney draw up an agreement specifying exactly what interests the cosigner has (none, except in the event you default). The agreement should specify what say she has in managing or selling the property (again, presumably none, unless you have a problem) and what percent of the profit she will receive in the event the property is sold (again, presumably none). This will help protect your interests.

Good credit is important in the world in which we live. You won't get a mortgage without it.

CREDIT QUIZ

	YES	NO
1. FICO produces credit scoring?	[ ]	[ ]
2. Underwriters tend to use financial profiling?	[ ]	[ ]
3. An "A" is the top credit category?	[ ]	[ ]
4. You can often improve your credit score?	[ ]	[ ]

	YES	NO
5. You can fix any bad credit?	[ ]	[ ]
6. Self-employed people have a harder time getting mortgages?	[ ]	[ ]
7. The less cash you put down, the better your chances of getting a mortgage?	[ ]	[ ]
8. It's a good idea to keep a month or two of cash reserves?	[ ]	[ ]
9. Bankruptcies and foreclosures are never forgiven?	[ ]	[ ]
10. The longer you've held a credit card the better?	[ ]	[ ]
11. It doesn't matter how much you owe on your credit card?	[ ]	[ ]
12. It doesn't matter how often you apply for credit?	[ ]	[ ]
13. Don't spoil your credit by refusing to pay a creditor with whom you're having an argument?	[ ]	[ ]
14. Lenders never accept your explanations?	[ ]	[ ]
15. You can never correct a credit report error?	[ ]	[ ]
16. No credit is almost as difficult to handle as bad credit?	[ ]	[ ]
17. Getting a cosigner might help you get a mortgage?	[ ]	[ ]

ANSWERS

1. Yes	7. No	13. Yes
2. Yes	8. Yes	14. No
3. Yes	9. No	15. No
4. Yes	10. Yes	16. Yes
5. No	11. No	17. Yes
6. Yes	12. No	

SCORING

14–17 You're probably a good credit risk.
10–13 You know what it takes to improve your credit.
 6–9 You may need some help with your credit.
 0–5 I'm not sure I'd loan you money!

10

Finding a More Affordable Mortgage

It's all well and good to talk about interest rates and whether a mortgage is for 15 or 30 years. But when you're struggling to afford a home, what's of most concern is the monthly payment. The monthly determines whether or not you can get into a home.

Why Should I Consider an Adjustable-Rate Mortgage?

A popular way of getting a lower monthly payment is to opt for an adjustable-rate mortgage. You can think of an adjustable-rate mortgage (ARM) as a more affordable mortgage, at least when buying the home. In exchange for the option of charging you a higher interest rate at a later date, a lender will give you a lower monthly payment today. But, of course, an initially lower monthly may be just what it takes to get you into the house you want.

Typical ARM
  $250,000 Fixed-rate loan at 7% = $1,663 monthly
  $250,000 ARM loan at 5% initial rate = $1,342 monthly

Because your payments almost always rise later on, some detractors call it a compact with the devil. Nonetheless, an ARM in some markets can cut your initial payments by as much as a third. That can mean the difference between being able to purchase and being left out in the cold. It's also why ARMs are traditionally referred to as more affordable mortgages.

In order to make an intelligent decision about whether an ARM is right for you, it's worthwhile to take a closer look at how they work. ARMs are the most sophisticated mortgages, yet there is nothing hard about understanding them.

How Does an ARM Work?

The best way to understand an ARM is to compare it to a fixed-rate mortgage.

With a fixed-rate mortgage you always know where you stand. Your interest rate and, hence, your monthly payment remain constant for the life of the loan whether it is for 3 years or 30 years.

With an ARM, it's quite different. Your interest rate fluctuates. It moves up and down depending on market conditions. Your monthly payment, which reflects the interest rate, likewise can vary up or down over the life of the loan.

Low Initial Rate: The Teaser

Given a choice between a mortgage where you never know what your monthly payment is going to be, and a mortgage where the monthly payment is fixed, any reasonable person would opt for the fixed-rate mortgage. It's a no-brainer.

Therefore, lenders have to sweeten the pot to entice borrowers to go for the ARM. The sweetener they use is the "teaser." This is an artificially low initial interest rate and, hence, a low initial monthly payment. The lender says in effect, "If you take the ARM, I'll cut your monthly payments at the beginning." That's quite an inducement. It's what makes this loan so affordable.

TIP

The real key to deciding whether or not to get an ARM is how long the teaser rate lasts. If you get an initial low interest rate and payment for just 1 month, and then it goes up, you've hardly accomplished anything. On the other hand, if the low monthly payment

lasts for several years, it can be just the right thing, particularly if you sell or refinance when the teaser expires.

The Consumer Strategy

The theory behind using an ARM for most consumers is twofold. First, you want the teaser to be for as long as possible so you get a lower monthly payment than you otherwise would get. Second, you hope that once the teaser evaporates and your interest rate and payment go up, you can refinance to another ARM with another low teaser [or if interest rates have fallen, to a low fixed-rate (and fixed payment) mortgage]. Thus, at least in theory, you can keep on going almost indefinitely with a low monthly payment.

TRAP

 Don't be shy about refinancing. Today lenders are increasingly willing to roll the typical refinance costs (between 2 and 5 percent of the mortgage) into a slightly higher interest rate. That means that if interest rates fall, you can often refinance at no cost to you. The main concern is that your mortgage amount does not rise and your monthly payments fall. Some people who bought ARMs refi just to get a $25 monthly payment reduction! To prevent that, many lenders are including prepayment penalties for refis in less than 3 years.

From the Lender's Perspective

It's worthwhile to take a moment to understand why a lender would want you to use an ARM or would entice you to get one with a teaser. The reason has nothing to do with altruism.

Thirty years is a very long time. Yet, that is the standard term of a real estate mortgage. The problem for the lender is that over the course of those 30 years interest rates can rise very high, particularly if there's an inflationary period.

When interest rates go up, mortgages with fixed low rates are worth less. (They operate just like bonds.) This adversely affects the lender's portfolio.

In order to reduce the risk of higher interest rates during inflationary times, lenders would like to be able to adjust the interest rates on their existing mortgages. They'd like to be able to raise the mortgage rates to reflect the higher market rates, thus protecting their portfolio. Hence, the concept of the ARM, the mortgage which allows the lender to raise rates.

The ARM is basically a device to protect lenders, not borrowers. However, because no reasonable borrower would freely give a lender the additional power of raising rates (and monthly payments), lenders are forced to give borrowers something in return—the teaser.

All of the back and forth between lender and borrower usually centers on how long that teaser lasts. The lender wants it for as short a time as possible. The borrower wants it for as long as possible.

TIP

Be sure you check out lots of different ARMs. Each lender has its own policy on the teaser. While one may offer it for only 3 months, another may offer it for 3 years.

The Basics of an ARM

Having gone into the tactics used by both borrower and lender on an ARM, let's now turn to how these mortgages actually work in practice. It's a somewhat arcane process.

Four Common Elements of an ARM

- An index
- A margin
- An adjustment period
- Steps

What Is an Index?

Since the interest rate (and monthly payment) of the ARM goes up and down, there must be some objective indicator to determine when and how much these fluctuations will be. (It wouldn't do to have the lender arbitrarily raise interest rates and payments on a whim!)

In order to determine what the interest rate is for an ARM, the mortgage is indexed. This means that the interest rate of the ARM is tied to some well-known economic measure that can't be influenced by the lender. Typical indices include Treasury bill rates of various lengths; the cost of mortgage funds to the lender; the cost of funds available to the borrower from government agencies; and other indices.

The way the index works is quite simple. If the index falls, the ARM's interest rate will fall. If the index rises, the ARM's interest rate will rise.

TIP

Lenders usually want their ARMs tied to indices that record volatility in the market. But borrowers usually want their ARMs tied to those indices that tend to move slowly, if at all. Finding the right index is one of the important features when selecting an ARM.

Stability of the index means that interest rates and monthly payments aren't likely to fluctuate too much. A volatile index means that your payments could be all over the board. For most borrowers, wide fluctuations in monthly payments are very hard to handle.

The agencies that regulate ARMs do not specify which index a lender must use. It's up to the lender to make this selection. The regulators only specify that the index must be one that the lender has no control over and must reflect interest rates in general and be widely publicized.

Most Common Indices

6-month Treasury

1-year Treasury

3-year Treasury

Bag of funds rate

Average cost of mortgage rates

Libor (London Interbank Offered Rate)

Treasury Securities Index

Published weekly by the Federal Reserve Board, it gives the interest rate for Treasury securities. This is the interest rate that investors pay to buy these government debts.

10-Year History

- Six-month T-bill—The 6-month T-bill is usually the most volatile of indices and most closely reflects current market conditions. The rate is established at weekly auctions.
- One-year T-bill—Also volatile. Based on the weekly average of daily yields of actively traded 1-year T-bills.
- Three- to five-year T-notes—Similarly volatile. Based on constant maturities.

Cost of Funds Index

Compiled by the Federal Home Loan Bank Board, this gives the average interest rate that member banks and savings and loan associations paid on funds during the previous period. It is reported monthly by district. It represents the cost to members (banks and savings and loans) of money if they have to borrow from the government.

History—stable, with less dramatic movements up and down. The most commonly used Cost of Funds index is the 11th district.

Average Cost of Mortgage Rate

This index consists of the average interest rate charged by major lenders for newly originated fixed- and adjustable-rate conventional mortgage loans on previously occupied homes. It is published monthly and is probably the most accurate assessment of changes in mortgage interest rates.

History—fairly stable. One of the less volatile measures.

Libor Rate

Almost no one outside of the lending industry has heard of the London Interbank Offered Rate (LIBOR) index. Yet, it is one of the oldest. It is also one of the most stable during most periods. In recent years, instability in the lending markets, however, have led it to become volatile. If you can find a lender who uses this rate, and if the margin is not unreasonable, it might be one of the best to use.

History—overall, stable.

When a lender offers you an index, it is required by law to show you the history of the index going back several years. Just be sure that the index history covers the volatile interest rate period of 1978 to 1982 and the 1990s. Those years will tell you more than most others about what this index is likely to do when interest rates change dramatically.

How Do I Pick an Index?

Obviously you can't pick an index. The lender does this. But you can shop for lenders until you find one who has the index most suited to your needs.

You want to pick a lender and an index that show some stability over time. But be careful. An index that is volatile may give you a better teaser rate and payment when it's down than an index that is stable, but up. But if times change, your payment could skyrocket.

TIP

Interest rates fluctuate up and down over time. The best time to get an ARM is when interest rates are high. That way, when they fall in the future, your payments are more likely to go down. The worst time to get an ARM is when interest rates are low. You are almost guaranteed of higher payments as interest rates rise in the future.

What Is a Margin?

The interest rate you pay on your mortgage is not simply the interest rate that the index reflects. Rather, the lender will add a "margin" to the index to determine your actual mortgage interest rate.

For example, the lender may specify in your ARM mortgage documents that the margin is 3 percent. That means that when the index is 4 percent, for example, the lender adds the margin of 3 percent to the 4 percent and you have an effective mortgage interest rate of 7 percent.

The margin is tied directly to the index used. If the index is generally low, the lender will tend to use a higher margin. If the index is generally high, the lender will tend to use a lower margin.

What Is an Adjustment Period?

After the index, the next critical feature to look at in an ARM is the adjustment period. How frequently can the lender adjust the mortgage rate up or down?

The adjustment period is arbitrary and each lender will specify what it wants in the loan documents. This is something you can pick and choose as the borrower only by switching lenders. Here are some of the more commonly used adjustment periods:

ARM Adjustment Periods

Monthly

Bimonthly

Three months

Six months

Annually

Biannually

Every 3 years

Every 5 years

To keep the teaser rate longer, you will want the longest adjustment period possible. This gives you the greatest period of low payments. However, lenders typically want the shortest adjustment time. This gives them the greatest protection against hikes in interest rates.

Therefore, when shopping for a mortgage, it is highly advisable to place the adjustment period as a big priority on your list of terms.

Hybrids

There are many hybrid mortgages. Some offer an adjustable rate for a few years, then can be switched to a fixed rate. Some are "called" (become due) in 7 years even though they are amortized (the monthly payments are spread out evenly) over 30 years. There are numerous variations all with their advantages and problems, and we will discuss these at the end of this chapter.

What Are Steps?

Many ARMs set a maximum limit on the amount the interest can be raised each adjustment period. For example, some ARMs have a 1 or 2 percent interest rate adjustment. That means that regardless of how the real interest rate has moved, the interest rate on the mortgage can only be adjusted in steps of 1 or 2 percent.

To see how steps work, let's say interest rates on our index have gone through the roof. Can an ARM mortgage rate go up in one adjustment period to accommodate the full interest rate hike? In other words, if the original interest was 5 percent and rates spike up by 5 percent, can the ARM's interest rate be raised by 5 percent (which would have the effect of almost doubling the monthly payment!)?

If the loan did not have steps, then the answer would be "Yes!" However, nearly all ARMs have steps that limit the hikes in the interest rate per each adjustment period. These limits are typically anywhere from ½ percent to 2½ percent per adjustment period. Thus, regardless of how much the mortgage index fluctuates, the interest rate cannot be hiked more than the step amount each period.

To get a better sense of how steps work, let's compare two different mortgages. The first has a step of 1 percent per adjustment period. The second has a step of 2 percent. Both mortgages have adjustment periods of 6 months.

When interest rates spike with the first mortgage, the interest rate on the mortgage goes up 1 percent after 6 months. After a year, it goes up to 2 percent.

With the second mortgage, the interest rate goes up 2 percent after 6 months and up to 4 percent after a year.

The result is that the increase on the monthly payment in the second mortgage is *twice* that of the first mortgage.

The point is that the smaller the steps, the greater the lag time accommodating a spike in interest rates. (Of course, a sudden decline would not be felt as quickly, either.) The result is far more stability in the monthly payment. It also means that there's going to be a greater time during which the teaser rate is likely to continue in effect.

ARM lenders are naturally concerned about the lag in mortgages with small steps. They see that they could lose out on revenue from interest when rates spike up. Naturally, lenders want the mortgage interest rate to keep pace with the index. They see that mortgages with small steps would lag behind, thus causing them to lose interest income. As a consequence, many ARMs are written with "catch-up" clauses. These clauses provide that even though the step doesn't rise fast enough to keep pace with the index, any interest lost to the lender in this fashion would be carried over to the next adjustment period.

With a catch-up clause in a mortgage, the beneficial effects of smaller steps are nullified over a long period of time. In the previous example, the mortgage with 1 percent steps would continue to increase toward the maximum even after the index had turned down. It would continue to rise until all of the increases in the rate had been given to the lender.

TIP

One answer for the borrower in a situation where there are large steps and/or catch-up clauses is to bail out of the mortgage and refinance. The one control the borrower has is to simply say, "Nope, I won't play this game anymore." The problem, of course, is that there may be a prepayment penalty for paying off the mortgage. Or your financial situation could change for the worse and you might not be able to refinance.

TRAP

Although catch-up clauses tend to nullify the beneficial effect of smaller steps in the long run, they don't do so in the short run. If you plan to sell the property fairly quickly, small steps—even with a catch-up clause—can prove beneficial, provided the lender doesn't tack on the catch-up interest to the mortgage payoff amount.

What Are Interest-Rate Caps?

One of the biggest problems with ARMs is the uncertainty that they produce. The borrower never really knows what his or her payments are going to be tomorrow. It's this uncertainty that causes many borrowers to forgo ARMs.

Lenders are aware of borrowers' fears of hikes in mortgage payments caused by unlimited interest-rate hikes on ARMs. If the mortgage were allowed to rise without restriction, in a very volatile market we might start up paying 7 percent and end up paying 15 percent or more. Our monthly payments could more than double as well! Few borrowers would take out a mortgage with such an unrestricted possibility.

To help reduce borrowers' fears, lenders frequently put an interest rate cap on the ARM. A *cap* is a limit on an ARM. It limits the amount the interest rate can rise (or fall). In this way the lender, appropriately, is assuming some of the risk in markets with extremely volatile interest rates. (If there was a 6 percent cap—the interest rate on the ARM couldn't rise by more than 6 percent—and if the market rate for interest rose by 10 percent, the lender would have to assume the loss of 4 percent in interest.)

The cap puts both a ceiling and a floor on the mortgage. The interest rate can't go above a certain amount. But it can't go below a certain amount either. If the cap is 5 percent, for example, the rate can rise above or fall below 5 percent of the current rate. But that amounts to a swing of 10 percent.

TIP

A mortgage with a 3 percent cap is a far better mortgage than one with a 5 percent cap. And a mortgage with a 2 percent cap is better than the others. While this may seem obvious, it nevertheless is a consideration that should be taken. What this means is that you should get the lowest interest-rate cap you can find.

What Are Mortgage Payment Caps?

In addition to setting a maximum cap on the interest rate of the mortgage, some ARMs also set a maximum limit on the amount the monthly payment can be raised each adjustment period regardless of what happens to the interest rate.

A monthly payment cap states that the payment cannot rise beyond a certain percentage of the previous period's payment. A common payment cap is 7.5 percent. The monthly payment in the new adjustment period cannot increase by more than 7.5 percent of the payment in the preceding period.

To see how payment caps work, let's say interest rates on your index have gone through the roof. You have a maximum step of 2 percent per adjustment period. So the lender raises the interest rate a full 2 percent.

However, you also have a cap on the mortgage payment. It can't be raised more than, for example, 7.5 percent each period. Here's what happens.

A Mortgage Payment Cap in Effect
$100,000 mortgage for 30 years with 7.5% payment cap.

Step = 2%   Required increase in mortgage payment = $151

Cap = 7.5% (of mortgage payment)

Maximum increase in mortgage payment = $66

Without the payment cap, the mortgage payment would rise $151. With the cap, the maximum increase is $66.

When interest rates rise dramatically, the monthly payment cap keeps the payment relatively stable. In the above example, the payment cap kept the payment from rising by an additional $85.

For borrowers who have affordability issues and are scrimping to make the monthly payment, the payment caps seem like a panacea. Get the payment cap and there's major protection. However, payment caps have a sinister side.

What Is Negative Amortization?

Negative amortization is something that is often hidden from view unless you know what to look for in the mortgage documents. Although the negative amortization terms are fully explained in those mortgages in which it occurs, many people simply don't understand the implications. Many of us still fail to see the dangers.

Negative amortization means that instead of the amount you owe going down, it goes up! Each month, instead of paying off some of the loan you add to it. You end up owing more than you originally borrowed and/or having a longer borrowing period. What I feel is even worse, you end up paying interest on interest.

Negative amortization typically comes about because your payments are capped and the cap is lower than the interest rate increases.

Wanting such caps, as you've seen, is only natural. You want to be able to control your monthly payment. Your big concern is that the monthly payment does not rise too swiftly. Typically, you have limited ability to increase your income. You are afraid that sudden large monthly payment increases could cause you to lose your property. You are seeking protection.

TRAP

Remember, a monthly payment cap does not limit interest rate increases. What a monthly payment cap does is to restrict that portion of the interest-rate increase that you immediately pay. The portion that you do not pay, however, does not go away. Rather, it is added to the mortgage at some point.

The key to understanding payment caps is to remember that the portion of the interest rate that is not reflected in the increased monthly payment does not disappear. It is added to the mortgage. Thus, it's not that you're getting away without paying it. You're getting away without paying it *now*. You will pay it over the term of the loan.

TIP

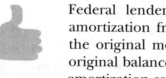

Federal lender regulations often prohibit negative amortization from increasing beyond 125 percent of the original mortgage balance. For example, if your original balance was $100,000, the maximum negative amortization can increase the mortgage is to $125,000.

Often an argument used by lenders to justify the bad effects of negative amortization is that housing price increases will more than offset it. Yes, we might be adding to the mortgage amount, but our house will be worth more anyhow, so why worry?

The hollowness of this argument comes from the fact that, although prices will most likely increase, negative amortization has the effect of giving that equity increase not to the borrower, but to the lender! You don't get more equity, you get more loan!

Should I Avoid Negative Amortization at All Costs?

No. It can be a necessary evil.

With affordability issues, your desire may be to control the monthly payment on your mortgage at all costs. You must keep it down. If this is your situation, and you're aware of what's happening, then negative amortization can simply be the penalty you pay for those lower payments. The key is that you're aware of what's happening.

TRAP

Be aware that mortgage payment caps are often a trade-off for other important benefits. A lender who offers a monthly payment cap as an inducement to a borrower often feels justified in asking for more restrictive terms in other areas. For example, such a lender may demand a prepayment penalty. If you pay off the mortgage early, it might cost you 6 months of interest! Since you will want the flexibility of getting out of the mortgage when the teaser rate is up, this could be a big drawback.

Should I Beware of Prepayment Penalties?

Yes, absolutely. Avoid them in mortgages. They do you no good. They are simply the lenders' attempts to lock you in—to keep you from bailing out of the mortgage when the teaser rate is up.

Always ask if the loan has a prepayment penalty. Until a few years ago, almost none did. Now lenders are increasingly trying to slip this in. Beware of it!

Caps Can Work against You

Ultimately, a mortgage with a monthly payment containing a cap may be higher than one without. Consider the following example, comparing cap rates with no cap, prepared from material offered by the Federal Home Loan Bank Board. In this case, various interest-rate caps are given and the monthly payment is shown over a period of 29 years. The chart assumes that interest rates start at 6 percent, then rise to 9 percent at year 5 and remain there. It also assumes that there is no interest-rate cap on the mortgage.

Cap Rate Comparison Chart

$100,000 30-year mortgage

		Monthly Payment			
Year	Interest Rate	7% Cap	7.5% Cap	10% Cap	No Cap
1	6%	$ 514	$514	$514	$514
2	7	540	552	565	572
3	7.5	567	594	622	630
4	8	595	638	684	689
5	9	625	686	753	748
6	9	656	738	753	748
10	9	797	800	753	748
15	9	1,018	800	753	748
20	9	1,112	800	753	748
25	9	1,112	800	753	748
29	9	1,112	800	753	748

Notice that the lower the monthly payment cap, the lower the monthly payments initially. But over the long run, the lower the monthly payment cap, the higher the monthly payments as the lender plays catch-up trying to recoup interest not received because of the payment cap. A 7.5 percent cap, for example, will result after year 10 in a payment of $800. Without the cap the payment would have been only $748.

Monthly payment caps can mean lower monthly payments now, but higher monthly payments later on if you hang onto the mortgage.

What If You Have Both a Monthly Payment Cap and an Interest-Rate Cap?

Some lenders use this combination and borrowers sometimes think that it is a significantly better loan. With the interest rate capped, the loan is indeed better for the borrower. But it is questionable as to how significant the benefit is when there is also a monthly payment cap.

To see why, look back at our previous example. Let's say that in addition to the monthly payment being capped, the interest rate was capped at a 3 percent maximum change with steps of 1½ percent a year. The chart would work out exactly the same! The interest-rate cap would have no effect since the interest rate only rose to the maximum (from 6 percent in our example to 9 percent) and the increases were never beyond the 1½ percent steps.

Only if the interest-rate cap were lower, in our example less than 3 percent, would it act to mitigate the negative effects of a monthly payment cap (something very unlikely).

When a mortgage has both an interest-rate cap and a monthly payment cap, you automatically should suspect that the interest-rate cap is set higher than the monthly payment cap and that negative amortization could take place. The reason is simple. If this weren't the case, if the interest-rate cap were set sufficiently low that no negative amortization could take place, then no monthly payment cap would be necessary.

What Are the Types of Adjustable-Rate Mortgages?

The most common is the straight 30-year ARM. However, there are many hybrids. The most common goes by the name of "fixed/adjustable," or by its term—3/30, 5/30, 7/30, or 10/30.

In these mortgages, you have a fixed rate for the first 3, 5, 7, or 10 years. Then the mortgage converts to an ARM at the then current interest rate for the balance of its 30-year term.

The purpose of this mortgage is to give you a more stable monthly payment combined with a slightly lower interest rate (and payment). The reason this is possible is that (from the lender's perspective) this is actually a 3-, 5-, 7-, or 10-year fixed-rate loan. This relatively short term affords the lender less risk over time than a standard 30-year payback and, thus, you get a lower interest rate and payment. Typically, the shorter the initial fixed-rate term is, the lower the interest rate and monthly payment. After the fixed-rate period, the loan reverts to a rather ugly ARM and the lender assumes that you will refinance.

TRAP

Some of these loans don't have the ARM at the end. You owe the entire unpaid balance at the end of the 3-, 5-, 7-,or 10-year period! This is a no-no for you as you never can know what your financial situation will be in the future. Without the automatic ARM attached (no qualifying, the loan simply rolls over), you might find yourself unable to refinance. Your choices would then be to quickly resell or lose the property to foreclosure!

What about a Convertible Option?

A convertible option is a mortgage with two different modes. The convertible blends adjustable- and fixed-rate features. You can get the big advantage of the adjustable-rate mortgage, lower initial interest rate, but you can also achieve increased stability over the life of the mortgage. For the lender, the convertible is a compromise. It doesn't lock the lender into a long-term fixed rate. On the other hand, it doesn't give the lender quite as much protection against volatility as the straight adjustable-rate mortgage.

A convertible mortgage is really like the fixed and adjustable we just discussed, only in reverse. You start out with an adjustable-rate mortgage. Then, after a set number of years, you are given the option of converting to a fixed mortgage (at then market rates).

For example, you might have an adjustable-rate mortgage with a low initial rate. It would be like any other ARM, except that perhaps in year 3, at your option, you could convert it to a fixed mortgage at the then current market rate.

TRAP

Some mortgages offer you this option for free. Others have a "conversion fee." Obviously the mortgage without the conversion fee is better from your perspective.

The big advantage of a convertible remains that it's another way to get a lower interest rate and, thus, a lower monthly payment. The lender gives you a lower rate because the mortgage is adjustable. Yet, you get the opportunity to convert to a fixed-rate mortgage later on. Most lenders offer convertible mortgages of one sort or another.

If you get a convertible, be sure you're very clear on when the conversion occurs. You may have a very small window of opportunity, say 3 months, to opt to convert to a fixed rate. If interest rates are high during that period, you would probably just pass. But if interest rates take a dip, that would be a most opportune time to exercise your option.

The value to you of a convertible loan comes from your ability to convert it to a fixed rate at some time in the future. If the conversion window happens to be during a period of lower interest rates, you can get into a fixed mortgage for very little cost.

Adjustable-rate mortgages are one more way of making the purchase of a home more affordable. In the next chapter, we'll look at special programs that national lenders offer that can sometimes be combined with ARMs to give you an even better deal.

AFFORDABLE MORTGAGES QUIZ

	YES	NO
1. Is an ARM usually a more affordable mortgage?	[ ]	[ ]
2. Should you go for a long-term "teaser" rate?	[ ]	[ ]

	YES	NO
3. With an ARM, is the strategy to hold long term?	[ ]	[ ]
4. All ARMs are tied to an index?	[ ]	[ ]
5. You normally want the most stable index?	[ ]	[ ]
6. It's to your advantage to get a short adjustment period?	[ ]	[ ]
7. It's to your advantage to get small steps?	[ ]	[ ]
8. An interest-rate cap can help protect you?	[ ]	[ ]
9. A monthly payment cap can lead to negative amortization?	[ ]	[ ]
10. Prepayment penalties area becoming more common?	[ ]	[ ]
11. Fixed/adjustable combos can be less stable?	[ ]	[ ]
12. A convertible loan doesn't allow you to change in midstream?	[ ]	[ ]

ANSWERS

1. Yes	6. No	11. No
2. Yes	7. Yes	12. No
3. No	8. Yes	
4. Yes	9. Yes	
5. Yes	10. Yes	

SCORING

10–12 You should be selling ARMs!

7–9 You need to recheck the advantages.

4–6 You need to recheck the disadvantages.

0–3 An ARM loan salesperson would love to see you coming!

11
Affordable Mortgage Programs

Who are the two biggest mortgage lenders in the country that offer mortgages as high as 103 percent of the purchase price?

If you started thinking of big banks, you'd be wrong. The two biggest lenders are Freddie Mac and Fannie Mae. These are quasi-public, private corporations that maintain a secondary market in home loans. When you get a loan through a mortgage broker or a bank (or a mortgage banker, which is a bank that only handles mortgages), chances are that the loan is sold to either Freddie Mac or Fannie Mae. The lender gets a fee for collecting your payments and now has money to loan on more mortgages. (Another giant secondary lender, Ginnie Mae, has announced plans to also enter this market more directly.)

In order to be able to "sell" your loan to one of these lenders, it must be "conforming." That means it must conform to the underwriting standards of Fannie Mae or Freddie Mac. (Remember, in Chapter 9 we talked about underwriting.) Here the lender you're dealing with gets you to fill out an application. Then the application and a credit report are submitted to either Freddie Mac or Fannie Mae. They take a look, along with your credit score, usually from FICO, and apply their own financial profiles. From this they issue usually a provisional approval or a rejection. If approved, you then can obtain one of the many different mortgage products they offer through lenders. Currently, the maximum loan is $307,000.

TRAP

Fannie Mae and Freddie Mae do not usually make loans directly to you, the borrower. Rather, you go through a direct lender or a mortgage broker.

It's hard to know just how much of the total home mortgage business in the country goes through these lenders. However, I have heard estimates as high as 50 percent. In any event it's a very large number, which is the reason that it's important to take a close look at the various affordable loans these two giants offer. (Remember, when we say *offer* we mean offer through conventional lenders, not directly.)

Fannie Mae and Freddie Mac set the maximum loan amount you can get (currently $307,000, however, this frequently is adjusted upward). They also determine what the FICO score is that will allow you to get prime loans (believed generally to be about 680 or so). They also have low-down and no-down programs as well as special programs for those who are credit-challenged.

Program Highlights

The various Fannie Mae and Freddie Mac programs go under a variety of names such as Affordable Gold 5 and Fannie 97. However, chances are you'll never hear these names. Rather, when you go through a bank or mortgage broker, you're likely to talk only about such vital matters as down payment and your income and credit requirements. Nevertheless, behind the scenes the direct and secondary lenders are very likely trying to fit you into one of these programs. The more you know, however, the more likely you are to find a program just right for you. For a more complete description of many of the Fannie Mae and Freddie Mac loan programs refer to Appendix B.

To get a sense of what's out there, let's go through some of the down payment, income, and credit requirements that these programs offer. You may be very surprised at how affordable they can be. (*Note:* Not all of the down payment, credit, and income requirements are for the same loan.)

Down Payment

When it comes to an affordable mortgage, 5 percent down is actually high. More typical are the 3 percent down programs—Affordable Gold 97 from Freddie Mac or Fannie 97 from Fannie Mae. Under these programs all you need to come up with is 3 percent of the purchase price. On a $200,000 home that's only $6,000, plus closing costs.

You don't have $6,000? Not to worry. Under some of the plans your down payment can be zero? That's right, you need put nothing down. Both lenders offer mortgage programs—Freddie Mac 100 and Fannie Mae Flexible 100—that can increase the mortgage amount to 100 percent.

But, you say, you don't have the money for the closing costs? Not to worry. These closing costs typically run about 3 percent for the buyer, and Freddie Mac will allow you to borrow that amount on a second mortgage. (Or, in some cases, the seller can put up the funds, you can receive them as gifts, or you can contribute them as "sweat equity" in the property.)

Is there a catch? Of course there is. You must have positively excellent credit. That typically means a high FICO score plus no recent delinquencies, bankruptcies, and foreclosures.

Uh oh, you have a problem? Well, there are plans for borrowers who are credit-challenged.

Credit Requirements

As noted previously, if you have good credit, a 100 percent mortgage may be within your reach. However, if your credit is less than sterling, then there are alternatives as well. Under Freddie Mac's Affordable Merit Rate and Timely Payment Rewards mortgage programs, you can get the property by paying a higher interest rate than would a person with great credit.

Typically, the low to no down payments still apply. However, there's a big extra incentive to these unusual mortgages. If you can make 24 consecutive payments on time, the interest rate (and consequently the monthly payment) will be cut. You'll end up paying less for the loan and the monthly payment! That's quite an incentive.

Of course, that doesn't mean you can get into this type of loan with terrible credit. Freddie Mac generally says that to qualify, while you can have some delinquent payments, you can't have more than two in the prior 12 months. However, you can have lots of other debt, *if* you can explain it in terms of divorce, medical emergency, job loss, or so on. Also, you can't have any bankruptcies within the previous 24 months and no foreclosures within the previous 36 months. Fannie Mae's rules are similar.

Sound too good to be true? Actually, these mortgages are designed for people who are good credit risks, but who simply have gotten into some financial trouble. They still let you buy a house. Keep in mind, however, that if you have truly bad credit, you won't be able to get any Fannie Mae or Freddie Mac mortgage.

Income Requirements

In the old days, at this juncture, I would insert a series of formulas that would indicate how much income you needed to qualify for a particular Freddie Mac or Fannie Mae loan. However, as indicated in Chapter 3 and elsewhere, today that's different. It's not just income that counts, but a combination of income, credit history, and down payment. It's all well and good to say that you probably can get one of these mortgages if your monthly payment will be no more than about 25 to 30 percent of your income; however, there are many other factors to consider. The only way to know for sure is to get yourself pre-approved by an underwriter, which is also covered in Chapter 3.

Having said this, when it comes to the affordable mortgage programs of both of these secondary lenders, sometimes it's more important to have less income than more! That's because these programs frequently are designed for those who are having trouble qualifying. They are designed to make homes affordable for those who otherwise could not buy them.

With many of the mortgage programs, you need to earn no more than the median income in your area (providing, of course, that the home is not priced too high) in order to qualify. Special exceptions are given for high-income areas. For example, you can typically earn 135 percent of the median income in Boston, 140 percent in California, and 170 percent in Hawaii.

What Are the Fannie Mae and Freddie Mac Loans?

As noted previously, they change all the time. Here's a list of some of the current loan programs:

Freddie Mac Affordable Loan Programs
   Affordable Gold 5

   Affordable Gold 3/2

   Affordable Gold 97

   Affordable Gold Alt 97

   Affordable Seconds

Fannie Mae Affordable Loan Programs
   Pledged Asset

   Timely Payment Rewards

   Interest First

   Other Programs

Where to Find Fannie Mae and Freddie Mac Loans

Interested? Go to Appendix B to see the specifics of some of these mortgage programs. Then, go to a mortgage broker or a banker to find out specifically what will work for you. You may be very pleasantly surprised!

12
Affordable Housing Programs

There are hundreds of special programs out there designed specifi-cally to help make homes more affordable. These usually take the form of assistance in getting a smaller or, in some cases, no down payment. They may also be in the form of a bigger mortgage at a lower interest rate with lower payments.

The variety of these kinds of programs and how they operate is enormous. Usually they require that you have good credit, but not always. In some cases, a short history of repayment of debt after a long history of poor repayment may be enough. In other cases, you may be able to get into the property with no money down or closing costs at all, but instead pay a slightly higher rent until you've accu-mulated enough cash for the down payment and closing (a lease option). In other cases, there are outright grants.

Many of these programs cater to the first-time home buyer. In those cases, you must prove that this is your first home. But, surpris-ingly, that's not as hard as it first may seem. Indeed, you may be a first-time home buyer even if you previously owned a home!

What Is a First-Time Home Buyer?

If you answered, reasonably enough, that it's a person who's never before bought a home, you'd be wrong, or at least not totally correct. According to most housing programs, and certainly those operated by the government, a first-time home buyer is usually someone who hasn't owned a home in the previous 3 years. If you owned a home 4

157

years ago, sold it, and haven't owned one since, you're defined as a first-time home buyer and many programs are open to you.

Most of the programs are administered by local city governments. In order to apply for them, you must contact the office of housing director (or whatever name your city uses). When you do, you'll be told of the type of program available, the qualifications, and how to apply for it.

For example, the city of Los Angeles offers a Mortgage Credit Certificate (MCC) to certain qualifying people. However there are strict household-size and maximum-income limits. (You can't make too much money and get in this program.) These figures change, and the program is subject to alterations or discontinuance.

You are also limited to purchasing a new house or existing home up to a maximum amount. Unfortunately, in the high-priced L.A. area, that tends to rule out homes in the more desirable areas.

The MCC gives the borrower a federal income tax credit of up to 20 percent of the mortgage interest. The credit reduces the taxes you pay and helps both in qualifying for a mortgage as well as in making the payments.

Other cities have similar programs. And there are a host of different types of programs that may be suited to other situations. For example, FEMA (Federal Emergency Management Agency) coordinates low-interest-rate loans to victims of natural disasters. The key, however, is that the federal government must declare the area in which your home is located an officially designated disaster area. Most states have similar programs.

In addition, HUD (U.S. Department of Housing and Urban Development) also offers a host of loans, some directly funded, to help with financing. Through the FHA (Federal Housing Administration) there are programs designed for those with little money to put down, for farmers, and for others. (See the following section on government loans.)

There also are literally hundreds of other organizations that offer financing for those in special circumstances.

How Do I Find Out about the Various Mortgage Programs?

You'll have to do the legwork. Most of the programs are government sponsored and that means calling, writing, and sometimes going down to government offices. Generally, you'll want the housing office director, but the title of the person may vary significantly.

TRAP

Most of these programs do *not* offer mortgages directly. Rather, they give tax credits, insure, guarantee, or otherwise help you get the mortgage. But you still have to go to a lender for the actual money.

Are There Any Special Fannie Mae Programs?

Yes, the giant secondary lender offers at least four special mortgage options to some of its standard mortgages (see Chapter 11 and Appendix B). These include the following:

FannieNeighbors.   It is designed for areas that HUD has designated as being underserved. In other words, it's for low- to moderate-income buyers located in minority census tracts or in central cities.

Community Land Trust.   This is another program that is for low- and moderate-income families. It involves nonprofit organizations that desire to acquire and hold land for the benefit of the community. The land trust takes title to the land and then sells homes under long-term ground leases, which offer affordable payments. A leasehold mortgage from a conventional lender is used instead of the standard mortgage.

Community Seconds.   This program offers second mortgages so that the home buyer needs less cash to get into the property. The mortgage is provided by federal, state, or local government agencies. It can even come from an employer. It can offer deferred payments or be forgivable.

Lease Purchase.   This program offers leases with an option to buy. A nonprofit organization would buy the home and then lease it to a home purchaser. Each month, part of the monthly rent payment would be set aside and later used for the down payment and closing costs. The buyer usually has 3 to 5 years to come up with the necessary funds for closing and down through the increased rent payments. These are then applied and the borrower assumes the existing mortgage on the property.

Contact. For more information on these programs as well as the location of lenders in your area, contact Fannie Mae at *www.homepath .com* or

Fannie Mae
3900 Wisconsin Avenue, NW
Washington, DC 20016
202-752-7000

What about the FHA?

The Federal Housing Administration was born out of the Great Depression to help Americans purchase homes. It provided some of the first long-term financing (20 years) the market ever saw.

Over the years it has undergone many changes. Today it's an arm of HUD, but it is still a big force in the market. Its great advantage, for those seeking an affordable housing solution, is that it provides low down payment financing. You can typically buy a home with 5 percent down, and in some cases as little as 3 percent down, using an FHA loan. (Its significance, however, has been diminished in recent years by affordable financing from Fannie Mae and Freddie Mac.)

Contact. For more information on HUD and FHA programs, contact the agencies directly in Washington, D.C., or at a state office.

HUD/FHA
451 Seventh Street, SW
Washington, DC 20410
www.hud.gov
www.hud.gov/fha/fhahome.html

How Do FHA Mortgages Work?

Unlike the secondary lenders we've been discussing in previous chapters, the FHA usually does not lend money directly. Rather, it insures lenders against loss. In other words, you get an FHA loan from a bank, through a mortgage broker, or from some other lender. If you default, the lender is protected. It will sustain no loss. The FHA will bear the burden.

TRAP

With such great protection, you'd think that lenders would be willing to offer lower-than-market interest rates on FHA loans. This, however, has rarely happened. Apparently, the lenders prefer to have their cake and eat it too.

FHA programs over the years have included the following:

Title I

    (b)   Financing purchase of mobile home units

Title II

203 (b)   Financing of 1- to 4-family units

203 (b)   Special veteran financing

207   Financing rental housing and mobile home parks

221 (d)   Financing low-cost, 1- to 4-family dwellings for displaced or moderate-income families

222   Financing one-family homes for service personnel

234 (d)   Financing condo projects and condo conversion projects

234 (f)   Financing condominium units

235   Assistance to low-income families to make home purchases by subsidizing mortgage interest payments

The FHA also has programs for second mortgages to help with home renovations. While not all of these programs are funded at any given time, the basic 203(b) program is still widely used to help families obtain mortgages. If you apply for an FHA mortgage, chances are that's the program you'll fall under.

Loan Limitations

There are a number of limitations to FHA loans that may make them impractical, depending on your situation. For one thing, the maximum loan amount is relatively low. It varies by area of the country. The maximum loan in low-cost areas is currently $115,200, in high-cost areas it is $208,800. (*Note:* These are changed on an irregular basis by the government so that the loan maximums in effect when you read this may be different.)

TRAP

In those parts of the country, such as the east and west coasts, where prices of homes have skyrocketed, FHA loans are virtually unknown because of their low maximum loan amounts.

Qualifying

There are special qualifying rules for FHA loans. Here are several of the most important.

Owner-Occupied.   In order to get the low down payment benefits of an FHA mortgage, you must plan to occupy the property. You cannot be planning to buy it and then rent it out.

TIP

FHA has a program for investors in which they can plan to rent out the property. The down payment is much higher, however, usually around 10 to 15 percent.

Approved Property.   In order to get an FHA loan, you must also get an FHA appraisal. This is supposed to be something quite a bit above the average appraisal. Not only is it supposed to give the market value of the property, but also give a clearance to the house indicating that it is structurally sound, up to current building standards, and free from damage done by wind, water, termites, fungus, erosion, and so forth. In other words, the house needs to get the FHA's stamp of approval.

While buying an FHA home in the past virtually guaranteed you were getting a sound property, this does not seem to be the case today. In talking with agents who run FHA loans on a regular basis, I've heard that the appraisal process is not much better than anyone else's. Indeed, the FHA has occasionally let serious problems go undisclosed. Therefore, while the appraisal is highly touted, I would not rely on it. I would instead suggest that you have a good professional home inspection.

Mortgage Insurance Premium.   In addition, to obtain an FHA loan you must buy mortgage insurance. This is not private mortgage insurance, as is obtained with most Fannie Mae and Freddie Mac loans, but special FHA mortgage insurance. You generally pay for it all up front at the time you get the loan. (The amount is an initial payment of 2.25 percent. However, if you take a course on home ownership and borrowing information, it can be reduced down to 1.75 percent.

Strict Qualifying.   The underwriting requirements for an FHA loan are not quite as strict as for other loans. For example, here are some of the more lenient qualities. You can probably get an FHA loan if

- At least 2 years have passed since a bankruptcy was discharged
- Any outstanding tax liens have been satisfied
- It's been 3 years since you had a foreclosure or deed-in-lieu of foreclosure
- All judgments against you have been paid

Other Advantages of FHA Loans

FHA loans may have other advantages that may not be fully apparent at first glance.

They May Be Partially Assumable

The ability to assume a loan is a huge feature when it comes time to sell. Today, for practical purposes, virtually no conventional (nongovernment insured or guaranteed) loans are assumable. That means that when you eventually sell your property, your current loan will need to be paid off and the next buyer will need to get a new mortgage.

Being able to assume the mortgage, however, means that the next buyer can take over your existing loan presumably with its current interest rate. If that rate is fixed at a level lower than the current market, it's quite a big plus.

Up until the mid-1980s, FHA loans were fully assumable. That meant that anyone could take them over without any qualifications. You could literally sell your home to a bum off the street, and he or she could assume the existing FHA loan.

The problems with such a system, however, are evident. Soon the FHA was awash with properties it had to take back as part of the lenders' foreclosure process. Indeed, at one point it looked as though the entire program might go under. So changes were made.

Today, anyone who wants to assume an FHA loan must pass a qualifying process at least as rigorous as the one the original borrower went through. This assures that whoever is responsible for repaying the loan has the wherewithal to do so. However, there is no reappraisal of the property.

Additionally, the seller may have some liability for 10 years after the sale. In other words, though you sell the home, if the buyer assumes the FHA mortgage and later defaults, you could be held at least partially liable. It makes sense to think twice about whom you sell the property to.

The good part is that the loan can be assumed, in many cases, at the original interest rate.

No Prepayment Penalties

These have never been allowed under the FHA program. If you want to pay off the mortgage, you can do so without the lender charging you a fee. Today that's not such a big deal. But years ago when conventional mortgages all had prepayment penalties, it was.

What Are Impounds?

When you get an FHA loan you are required to pay your tax and insurance as part of the monthly mortgage payment. In order to facilitate this, the lender will create and impound an escrow account, which means setting aside part of the payment. It will collect roughly one-twelfth of your taxes and insurance costs each month and then will make timely payments on them.

Veteran Mortgages

The VA (Veterans Affairs) also has a program to provide mortgages, often with no down payment. The key, of course, is that you must be a veteran to participate.

Over the years, hundreds of thousands of veterans have participated in this program. Indeed, it has provided the only affordable housing alternative for many of them.

How Do I Know If I Qualify?

Obviously you know if you're a veteran. However, you had to be on active duty status for a minimum number of days during specific periods of time to qualify.

The VA is constantly changing the qualifying periods. Therefore, your safest bet is to check directly with them. (Contact the Veterans Affairs office at *www.homeloans.va.gov.*)

If you qualify, you'll be given a certificate of eligibility. This can be used to get your "entitlement," which is the amount the VA will cover. (The VA guarantees the top portion of the loan to lenders.) Under current entitlements, this means that you can get a VA loan for 100 percent of the cost of the home up to a maximum of about $240,000.

TIP

You can take your entitlement with you. For example, if you buy a home using a VA loan and later sell it, paying off the loan, you can contact the VA to have your entitlement reissued. You can then use it to purchase yet another home. If, however, you allow someone else to assume your loan (discussed below), you could lose your entitlement.

How Do I Qualify for a VA Loan?

There are a number of requirements including the following:

- Veteran's entitlement
- Demonstrate a history of good credit

- Have sufficient income to make the payments as well as support your family

- You must intend to occupy the property. You cannot intend to rent it out as an investment. However, the property may be larger than a single-family home, for example, a duplex. In that case, you must intend to occupy one unit.

How Do I Get a Mortgage?

Like the FHA, the VA rarely makes any direct loans. Rather, it guarantees mortgages made by private lenders. This part is slightly different from the way the FHA works.

The VA charges a funding fee to the veteran depending on the amount put down. That fee is typically between 2 and 2.75 percent, although it can be reduced to as low as 1.25 percent if you put as much as 10 percent down.

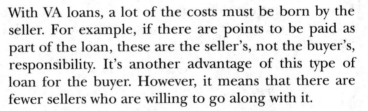

TIP

With VA loans, a lot of the costs must be born by the seller. For example, if there are points to be paid as part of the loan, these are the seller's, not the buyer's, responsibility. It's another advantage of this type of loan for the buyer. However, it means that there are fewer sellers who are willing to go along with it.

TIP

In the past, the VA has been amazingly flexible with regard to its loans. This is particularly the case for veterans who could not make the cut financially, but who made personal appeals. It's something to consider.

Does the House Have to Qualify?

Yes, it does. And the seller has to agree to go along with the many vagaries of a VA sale.

In order to obtain a loan, the VA must appraise the property. Based on the appraisal it issues a CRV (Certificate of Reasonable

Value). The loan is based on the CRV, not the sales price. The VA requires that the sale contracts specifying that the buyer is obtaining a VA mortgage, also allow the buyer to withdraw from the sale without penalty if the home does not appraise for enough in the CRV.

If the home appraises for too little, the veteran can still make the purchase, but must put up cash between the difference of the CRV and the sales price.

Selling a House with a VA Loan

When you sell your home, if you pay off the loan (the buyer obtains new financing), you can retain your entitlement and use it on another property as noted above. However, you may also have the new buyer assume your existing VA mortgage. In that case, the new buyer need not be a veteran. Anyone can make the assumption. This can be a big plus when selling the property, if you happen to have a big low-interest loan.

However, there is a catch. Your liability continues, even if you have someone else assume the loan. If that person later defaults and the home is foreclosed upon, you could be held personally liable by the VA for any loss it happens to sustain.

TIP

If the person who buys your property and assumes your VA loan happens to also be a veteran, you can have that person make a full assumption of liability. In other words, they can use their entitlement to take over your loan. And you would be out from under it.

Are There Impounds?

As with FHA loans, when you get a VA loan you are required to make your tax and insurance payments as part of the monthly mortgage payment. The lender will create an escrow account and impound part of the monthly payment. It will collect roughly one-twelfth of your taxes and insurance costs each month and then will make timely payment on them.

Contact. To find out if you're eligible for a VA loan and for other information, contact the Veterans Affairs office at *www.homeloans.va.gov.*

Other Contacts

See the contact information noted earlier in this chapter. For FEMA, information on mortgage programs is usually widely disseminated at and around disaster sites such as earthquakes, fires, floods, and so on. You can also contact FEMA directly at:

FEMA
500 C Street, SW
Washington, DC 20472
www.fema.gov

Also check with Fannie Mae and Freddie Mac for any programs they may be administering at:

Fannie Mae
3900 Wisconsin Avenue, NW
Washington, DC 20016
202-752-7000
www.fanniemae.com

Freddie Mac
8200 Jones Beach Drive
McLean, VA 22101
703-903-2000
www.freddiemac.com

For city and county programs, your best bet is to first contact the general information number and then ask for "housing." You'll have to work your way through to the person who handles special programs in your area.

AFFORDABLE HOUSING QUIZ

		YES	NO
1.	You can't learn about most affordable housing programs through your local city housing office?	[ ]	[ ]
2.	Fannie Mae does not offer special housing programs?	[ ]	[ ]
3.	The FHA guarantees mortgages?	[ ]	[ ]
4.	The VA insures mortgages?	[ ]	[ ]
5.	You can always get an FHA mortgage even though you have terrible credit?	[ ]	[ ]
6.	The VA doesn't care what the veteran pays for the home?	[ ]	[ ]
7.	The VA usually loans directly?	[ ]	[ ]
8.	FHA loans have no mortgage premium?	[ ]	[ ]
9.	VA loans avoid impounds?	[ ]	[ ]
10.	FEMA offers no loans?	[ ]	[ ]

ANSWERS

1. No	6. No
2. No	7. No
3. No	8. No
4. No	9. No
5. No	10. No

SCORING

5–10 You're a good candidate.

1–5   If you answered yes to any of these, you could have trouble qualifying under any of the special affordable mortgage programs.

13

Find an Agent Who Will Work with You

Agents love to work with serious home buyers. They know that if only they are loyal and persistent, they will be able to sell a home to the buyer and earn a commission. Agents, however, are somewhat less sanguine about working with buyers who have affordability issues. Here, the agent knows that there could be lots of time spent looking, many offers made and rejected, and in the end, the buyer might just get discouraged and no sale made. In short, a commission is anything but a sure bet.

If you're having trouble finding funds for the down payment and/or closing costs, making the monthly payments, or have a credit problem, then you may also find that you're having trouble getting an agent to do your bidding. You may not be able to find an agent who will stick with you through thick and thin until you find just the right house. In fact, once they learn of your situation, agents may be shying away from you.

Why Should I Care about Agent Loyalty?

What difference does it make if you're going through agents as fast as some people change shirts. It's not costing you anything, is it?

No, it may not be costing you in terms of dollars and cents. But lack of agent loyalty may keep you from finding just the house you want and need.

Agent loyalty means that the real estate agent will keep looking for you no matter how long it takes, even if that's a month, 6 months, or a year. This agent will not abandon you if you don't buy after a couple of home tours.

The agent will continue to look for homes for you in neighborhoods where it may be very difficult to find a property you can afford, not pressure you to look in lesser neighborhoods where you might not want to reside.

Your loyal agent will help you to get financing that might otherwise seem impossible to find, not dump you when you get your first turndown from a lender.

The agent will support you in your endeavors to find an affordable house that you'll feel proud to own. If there are affordability issues, you need a loyal agent to work for you.

How Do I Find a Loyal Agent?

It's an interesting question, since most times it goes the other way. Agents are always looking to find a loyal buyer, someone who will stick with them.

The one thing that agents hate more than anything else is the disloyal buyer, one who flits from one broker to the next. The agent may spend days searching out properties and more days showing them to the buyer. Over the course of several months, the agent may spend countless hours to the buyer's benefit only to discover in the end that the buyer purchases through a different agent! The agent's time has been wasted. Worse, it's time that might have been spent more productively on a more loyal buyer.

TIP

Remember, the agent doesn't get paid a commission unless and until the buyer makes a successful purchase.

This is not said to make you pity the poor real estate agent, but rather to give you the agent's perspective. Now the tables are somewhat turned and you need an agent to stand in your corner to help you find that one good property.

Thus, the first way you maintain agent loyalty is to give it in return. If the agent recognizes that you're sticking with him or her, chances are you'll be rewarded with loyalty in return. That agent may go the extra mile to help you out. The rule is, be loyal to your agent. And expect loyalty in return.

Will All Agents Return Loyalty?

Unfortunately, not always. Agents are very practical. If they begin to sense that you're not going to buy soon, they may simply decide that it's more worthwhile for them to spend their time on a more immediate buyer. Remember, they live on their commissions. If it takes you 6 months to find a home and another buyer 1 month, that's potentially six commissions they could make during the time it takes you to earn them one.

Therefore, you need to be practical, too. You need to make it plain to the agent that you don't expect them to spend 70 hours a week working on your cause. A couple of hours will do. You fully understand that the agent has to earn a living and if you can't find a house to buy right away, you're willing to be the buyer on the back burner. At least as long as the agent doesn't forget about you.

An agent may be working with half a dozen buyers at any given time. You have to be willing to accept the fact that one or another of those buyers may be "hot" and the agent will be devoting most of his or her time to getting an immediate sale. There's nothing wrong with that, as long as the agent continues to work on your behalf and, as soon as he or she finds a suitable property, puts you back at the front of the pack.

This is not to say that you need be a real estate stepchild. Perhaps an example will help put the situation in perspective.

You learn that, based on the funds you have and the mortgage for which you can qualify, the maximum price you can pay for a home is $135,000. You're definitely willing to spend that much.

However, you simply don't want to live in the neighborhoods in your area where the homes sell for $135,000. The minimum neighborhood you will consider has homes that start at $150,000.

Your agent may be sympathetic. He or she may even carry in one or two lowball offers in the better neighborhood that get rejected for being too low. But pretty soon your agent turns to you and says, "You need to be realistic. You're not going to find a home for $135,000 in a neighborhood where homes go for $150,000. Let's look in a cheaper area."

Now what do you do? If you go along with the agent, yes, very likely you'll quickly find a home you can afford to buy. The only trouble is, it won't be where you want to live.

So you must make it clear to the agent that you understand that it's unrealistic to think you'll *quickly* get a home in the more expensive neighborhood. But it's certainly not impossible. Fixers come onto the market. Highly motivated sellers appear. There are always Repos (repossessions) and REOs (real estate owned by lenders). You're willing to wait. Then you have to ask the agent if he or she is willing to work with you over the long haul.

At that point you'll find out how loyal your agent is. Many excellent agents will say they're sorry, but they have to earn a living, too. You're just not going to find a house with your attitude. They'll wish you well and say goodbye.

Keep in mind that these are not unsuccessful agents. Indeed, these are the agents who, very likely, make big commissions because they only work with the hot clients, those who will buy tomorrow.

If that happens, then it's time to move on. You want to find an agent who says, "Sure, I appreciate your situation. I'll devote as much time as I can. I'll have to work with other clients who will buy quicker, but I will continue to look for you, will show you every possible home that comes on the market, and (most importantly) will continue to take in your offers, even if they lowball the sellers."

TRAP

I've said it before, but it bears repeating. You may need to make 10 or more lowball offers before you get one accepted. But agents don't like taking these in. It's usually an affront to their ego each time an offer is rejected. You need an agent who simply sees it as business, and doesn't get ego involved.

Okay, so what if your agent cuts you loose? You were looking for an agent when you found this last one. You'll just keep on looking.

How Do I Interview an Agent?

If you need to find a good, loyal agent, the way to begin is by interviewing agents. There is no shortage of them. Just let it be known that you're interested in buying a house and they will come by to see if you're a hot buyer. Now you need to qualify them to see if they're suitable for your specific needs. Here's what you do.

Determine If the Agent Is Experienced

The last thing you need is to get an agent who just got licensed and wants to learn on you. Yes, this agent may indeed be willing to take extra time on your account, mainly because he or she doesn't have any other clients! You want an agent who's been around the block, who knows how to find properties and get offers accepted. Typically this means someone who's been in the field for at least 5 years. Just ask an agent you're interviewing how long he or she has been selling real estate. Most won't hesitate to tell you the truth.

Make Sure the Agent Is "Active"

In real estate, it's not uncommon to find inactive agents. These are people who have a real estate license, but don't actually make a living in the business. Instead, they may be retired from another career and simply trying to earn a few bucks selling property. There's nothing wrong with this. It's just that these part-timers often aren't on top of the market. And they may be hesitant about taking in offers, and even about working with active agents. You want a full-time, active agent on your case.

TIP

It's okay if the agent doesn't devote full-time just to you. What you want, however, is an agent who devotes full-time to real estate. You want to avoid an agent who spends a couple of hours a week in the office and, as a result, doesn't really know the market or how to deal with sellers.

Be Sure the Agent Knows the Area

This is more important than it may at first seem. All real estate is local. By that I mean that an agent can only know the property in his or her local area. A New York City agent may be useless in New Jersey (and not just because of different licensing) and vice versa. An agent who knows the Denver market will likely have no idea what's happening in Boulder or Colorado Springs. A San Francisco agent will be lost in Oakland, even though it's just eight miles across the bay.

TRAP

An agent's territory should actually be quite small, perhaps a few square miles or a portion of a city. Be wary of agents who tell you they can sell property anywhere in the state. They can, but that doesn't mean they know the market outside of their locale.

Indeed, perhaps the biggest attribute of a good agent is the precise knowledge he or she brings of a specific area. They know the names of the streets, the neighborhoods, and the builders. They know the schools, the crime statistics, and public services. Off the top of his or her head, this agent can tell you which property sold on what street, when, and for how much. That's what you're looking for. Once you identify a particular area or group of neighborhoods, you want an agent who knows them like the back of his or her hand. This agent won't waste time learning. He or she can tell you immediately what's available and how and where to get just the property you want.

Challenge your prospective agent. You've probably learned a couple of things about the neighborhood, perhaps a house that sold on a particular street last month. Ask the agent about it. Does he or she know of the house, the street, and the neighborhood? If it turns out you know the area better than they, it's time to look for another agent.

Be Sure Your Agent Can "Close"

Closing means making the sale. This is not to say that a super salesperson can close every deal. They can't. Some deals can't be made, particularly when you're lowballing the seller. But, *if* the deal can be made, you want to be sure that your agent can make it.

I recall one agent I knew who thought she was a hot shot. She would tell her buyer clients that she would get their offer accepted or no one would. However, when it was time to close the deal, when she was negotiating with the seller and his or her agent, she was a cream puff. She had no idea when to give and when to be firm, when to insist on a price and when to compromise. Hence, she only closed the easy deals.

Ask your agent how he or she will deal with a seller? See what they say. The answer can be instructive. An agent who can close will talk about such things as identifying objections and turning them around into positives. About sticking with it, and wearing the sellers down. At some point, talk about giving an ultimatum "that they can't refuse" and so on. In other words, an agent who can close will talk about closing.

On the other hand, if your agent talks about being polite to the seller, about giving them enough time to decide, about not making them angry so they'll reject your offer, consider getting another agent.

TRAP

A sure sign of an agent who can't close is when he or she insists that you must give the sellers plenty of time to decide on the offer, 2 or 3 days at least. This is a no-no. You never want to give the sellers a lot of time. The sellers might talk themselves into and out of the offer during that time. Another, better offer might come in and squeeze yours out. The ability to use time to your advantage is one of the biggest assets a good agent has. You want your agent to say something like, "we'll give them till midnight to decide" and it's 6 p.m. when he or she says it. This agent has the confidence in his or her ability to close the deal.

Make Sure Your Agent Is Completely Honest

Most agents are. But a few bad apples can go a long way toward spoiling the field for many. Honesty is hard to determine until you've been around a person for awhile. Watch out for misstatements. Exaggeration is one thing, but if the agent tells you something about a house that you later learn is totally untrue, it's time to move on.

One tip-off of a dishonest agent is if he or she boasts about cheating or in someway deceiving another buyer or a seller. Sometimes the agent will say such a thing to imply that you're in good hands because they know how it's done, but would never do it to you. However, my experience is that an agent who cheats one person will have no scruples when it comes to cheating another, such as you. You want someone who goes out of his or her way to be sure that no one who's party to a deal is injured.

Your Agent Should Be a Member of Trade Organizations

It almost goes without saying that your agent should be a Realtor®, which is a member of the National Association of Realtors, the largest national real estate trade organization. This should also entitle your agent to be a member of your local MLS (Multiple Listing Service), which handles cobroked listings. These are listings that all the agents in the area work on. And your agent should be a member of the local Real Estate Board, which often administers the MLS.

Get Recommendations on Your Agent

If you don't know an agent, get someone to recommend one. A personal reference from a relative, friend, or coworker can at least set you in the right direction. Once you locate the agent, ask him or her to supply you with half a dozen recommendations of previously satisfied customers. (That should be easy to do for someone who's been in the business several years.) Then call several of them. Find out how long the agent worked with them. Were they "hot" buyers or did they have affordability issues? The most important question to ask is, "Would you use this agent again?" Hopefully, they'll all say an unqualified, "Yes!"

Should You Work with a "Buyer's Agent"?

Historically, agents in real estate worked with both buyers and sellers. One of the most common ways of finding an agent, in fact, was to stop by an open house. The agent sitting at the open house would begin chatting with you and before you knew it, you had an agent to work with.

TIP

Sellers always want agents to hold open houses for them. They think that will help sell their home. However, studies have repeatedly shown that an open house primarily helps an agent find buyers *for other homes.* Don't be surprised if you stop by an open house and the agent tries to pick you up as a client. That's what he or she is mainly there to do.

Is there a conflict, however, if you're working with an agent who represents the seller of a home? How can the agent truly represent both the seller and you—the buyer?

When an agent lists a home, he or she normally becomes the agent of the sellers. That means that this agent's purpose is not only to find a buyer, but to get as high a price and as good terms as possible for the sellers. Of course as a buyer, that's exactly the opposite of your interests. You want the lowest price and the best terms for you.

But you may be thinking that many times you work with agents who are not actually the lister of a particular home. Aren't they on your side?

Not necessarily. As subagents of the lister, they may owe their bond of loyalty, their fiduciary relationship, to the sellers as well. In other words, every agent you may be dealing with may actually be an agent of the seller! You might have no one in your corner.

How Do I Determine Whom My Agents Represent?

The answer is simple—ask!

The way to find an agent who represents you, and not the sellers, is to ask whom the agent represents. The agent may declare either for the sellers, or for you, or in some cases for both.

TRAP

Don't get hung up on who pays the agent. Typically the seller pays the agent. But this does not necessarily mean that the agent represents the seller. The agent can declare for either party, and who pays him or her doesn't matter. Just because the seller pays the agent doesn't necessarily mean the agent represents the seller.

Today in many states, before you make an offer the agent must present you with a written declaration stating who he or she represents. Take this statement to heart. If the agent represents the sellers, be careful. Anything you say can and will be used against you!

For example, if you offer $200,000 for a property, yet tell a seller's agent that you're really willing to pay $220,000, that agent is required to tell the seller that you're willing to pay more. When that happens, just how seriously do you think the sellers will treat your $200,000 offer?

On the other hand, if you are working with a buyer's agent, that agent is required *not* to tell the seller your top price. On the other hand, if your buyer's agent discovers that the sellers are willing to take $10,000 less than the asking price, the agent is required to tell you that fact!

It's easy to see why it's beneficial to work with a buyer's agent.

Sometimes an agent will declare that they represent both buyers and sellers. This is often the case when it's the same agent who both lists the property and submits your offer. There is nothing legally wrong with this. Indeed, in the strange ethics of business, there is nothing ethically wrong with it as well. However, for my money, it's simply a theoretical fabrication that makes no common sense.

No slave can serve two masters, and no agent can represent both buyers and sellers as well as an agent who declares for just one of the parties. That's why if you're working with a dual agent (one representing both buyers and sellers), be on your guard. Don't count on the agent always being in your corner.

You may want to work with a dual agent, however, in order to get a savings on the commission. An agent who represents both buyers and sellers doesn't have to split the commission with other agents and may be willing to cut a deal with you for a portion of the commission (in the form of a reduced price).

Will a Buyer's Agent Represent Me Better?

There's a second reason for using a buyer's agent. You probably will be shown a bigger spread of properties. The reason is that ultimately, a buyer's agent relies on you for the commission, not the seller. (If this is a shock, hold on. We'll go into this in greater detail.)

A buyer's agent is willing to show you all sorts of properties, including those that may be for sale by owner and others that the sellers are thinking about listing, but haven't yet signed an agreement. The buyer's agent may also show you bank-owned properties (repossessions), in which the bank is selling and not offering to pay a commission to brokers. A seller's agent generally will only want to show you listed properties, ones that he or she can more easily collect a commission on.

Of course, it all depends on how good the buyer's agent is and what contacts he or she has. Some buyer's agents are nothing more than seller's agents wearing a different coat. Others really do go out of their way for the buyers.

Do I Really Have to Pay a Buyer's Agent?

In theory, yes. But as a practical matter, probably not. Most buyer's agents find a way to get the seller to pop for the commission. Thus, you get the benefit, but without the expense.

On the other hand, there's always the chance that the buyer's agent will find a property for you that's just perfect, but the seller is unwilling to pay a commission. Then what happens?

If you're struggling to buy a home, the last thing you need is to have the additional expense of a commission. A buyer's commission is typically half of a regular commission. If the full commission is 6 percent, we're talking 3 percent. On a $200,000 that's a whopping $6,000, over and above the down payment and the closing costs!

Whoa! I'm sure many readers are back peddling very fast. The last thing they want is to owe another huge amount of cash. But let's take it slowly.

First, the chances are excellent that the seller will pay the commission. Most sellers realize they'll need to pay a commission and there's usually very little quibbling between agents about splitting it.

Second, you don't have to take the house *if* the seller won't pay and the commission is up to you. For the once or twice odd chance that this will occur, simply pass.

Finally, if this is in fact the perfect home for you and no other will do, *and* the seller won't pay the commission, then you can negotiate with your buyer's agent. For example, the agent may be more than willing to accept a second mortgage in lieu of cash. You could pay it off over a period of years.

Or the agent may be willing to accept a second mortgage with a partial payment and the understanding that no further payment will be made until you eventually sell the property. In other words, the agent gets the majority of the commission when you resell.

Or else whatever other terms you might agree upon. Maybe the agent will accept a boat or motorcycle in lieu of the commission!

The point is don't be terrified of owing a commission to a buyer's agent. It will probably never come to pass. And if it does, there are many ways out.

Should I Sign a Buyer's Agent Agreement?

A true buyer's agent may want you to sign an agreement in which you agree to pay him or her a commission for finding you a property. It's sort of like a listing agreement, only instead of listing property it's listing you.

Many buyers, having lived for decades under a system where the sellers always paid the commission, are quite taken aback by this. Nevertheless, it's something at least worth considering, particularly if the buyer's agent can get you the house you want at a significant savings.

Remember, in most cases the commission is still paid by the sellers. Usually what happens is that if the property is listed, the buyer's agent works out a "cobroking" deal with the seller's agent for half of the listing commission. The commission to you is zero. That's the way it works in most cases, but not all.

For that reason, it's very important you carefully read any agreement a buyer's agent wants you to sign. You should particularly be on the watch for:

- Anything that says you must pay the buyer's agent an up-front fee. Some agreements state that you will pay the buyer's agent $1,000 (more or less) to commence finding a property for you. If you eventually buy, the advance is taken from the commission. If you don't, you lose the money.

There are several problems here, beyond the obvious one of having to take money out of pocket. The first is that once you pay the money, you're unlikely to dump the agent, even if he or she does a terrible job. If you dump the agent, you lose the advance. So you're tied in.

Second is that you are actually discouraging the agent from working hard. Why should the agent work to find you the perfect property if he or she has already been paid? Indeed, this agent could make a living simply by going around and collecting advance fees.

Third, getting an advance fee discourages an agent from working hard to get paid by the seller. You want a hungry agent who will demand the seller pay a fee and demand that the seller's agent split that fee. If the agent thinks you're a pushover for collecting a commission, how hard do you think he or she will work?

- Another concern here is that the buyer's agent could potentially get two commissions, one from you and another from the sellers.

- There's also the matter of commitment. You obviously want the agent committed. But how committed to the agent does the contract make you? Any demand that you work exclusively with the buyer's agent for an indefinite or a long period of time should be suspect. Just as with a listing agent, it's not unreasonable for a buyer's agent to want you to work exclusively with him or her in finding a house. After all, why should they spend a lot of time looking for you if you then simply hop over and purchase through a different agent? As we've emphasized, if you want to work with a buyer's agent, you should give them your loyalty whether it's in a contract or not.

On the other hand, your loyalty should have a time limit. If the agent, for example, can't find the house of your dreams for you within 60 days, you should have the right to look using someone else.

A good time limit when listing a home with a buyer's agent is 30 to 90 days, particularly if you have affordability issues and this is an agent who you feel will really put forth the effort on your behalf.

- Finally, there's the matter of the commission itself. You don't want the agreement to specify that you have to come up with cash for the agent. You want it to say that you'll negotiate. You also want it to be very specific that if you don't buy the house, there's no commission owed.

Without a formal agreement, you can simply drop the buyer's agent and work with someone else. With a formal agreement, it's not

so simple. While the agreement is in force, you could owe the
buyer's agent a commission even if you buy through another agent
and even if you buy directly from the seller with no agent involved!
As I said, be sure you carefully read any agreement before you sign
it. Take it to an attorney for clarification.

Should I Ever Work with More Than Just One Agent?

I've gone out of my way to emphasize that you should put loyalty
above all else with an agent. But I'm sure some readers are wondering if there aren't circumstances where working with more than one
agent will pay off?

The answer is yes, but rarely. Every so often you'll come across an
agent who doesn't cobroke. In other words, this agent won't cooperate and split a commission with other agents.

Agents who belong to multiple services are usually supposed to list
all homes with the service and make them available to all other
agents as soon as possible. Listing the property and holding it off the
market by not letting other agents know about it is called keeping a
"vest pocket listing" and is usually considered unethical behavior. (It
benefits the agent, but is usually detrimental to the seller, the agent's
fiduciary.)

Nevertheless, sometimes agents do hold properties away from
other brokers, sometimes with the seller's permission. Your only
choice here is to pay a buyer's agent, as described above, to negotiate for this property or to deal directly with the seller's agent.

Similarly, a situation may arise with a FSBO where the seller refuses to pay a commission. Your choices are to pay the commission
yourself or to deal directly with the seller.

Either way, it's not a good situation, but sometimes it does happen. And when it does, you need to use your best judgment.

Should I Work with a Salesperson or a Broker?

It really doesn't matter. Both are licensed (or should be!) in every
state. A salesperson is someone who must work under a broker's

tutelage until he or she gains enough experience to go out on his or her own (usually a couple of years). A broker is one who can open an office and act on their own when selling real estate.

Confusion enters the arena when brokers sometimes defer to other brokers and work as salespeople. This commonly happens when a broker doesn't want the expense, risk, and headache of operating his or her own office. They'll hang their license under another broker and work as a salesperson.

If you're not sure, just ask. Whomever you're dealing with will quickly tell you what their status is. What's important is that the person you're dealing with passed the tests we described earlier and is able to fully serve you.

TIP

The word "agent" refers to anyone who sells real estate for a commission, whether a broker or an agent. The word Realtor® refers to a broker member of the National Association of Realtors.

Should I Work with an Independent Agent or One Who Represents a National Company?

Again, it's not critical either way. Real estate is a personal kind of business, so the person with whom you're dealing is more important than the company.

However, it's important to understand that the big company can be important too. If something goes wrong in a deal, it's nice to know that there's a huge entity standing behind your agent.

TIP

In order to sell real estate, a broker must be licensed in a state. Thus, when we talk about "national" real estate companies, we're mainly talking about franchises. The national company gives a local broker a franchise to use their name and everything that goes with it. The broker pays a franchise fee for this. Of course, there are some wholly owned real estate brokerages within a state, so you could be dealing with a "company store." Ask to find out.

One of the drawbacks of using a broker who works for a national company is that you may be limited because of their policies. The company may have very specific requirements when it comes to commission, how an agent is to work with a buyer, and even how many clients an agent should have.

If you have affordability issues, and you need to work out a unique deal with your agent, a national company's policy requirements may get in the way. The agent may need to be continuously going back for approval of this or that, which may not be forthcoming.

The most important thing when working with an agent is that you feel comfortable with that person and that the agent be honest and competent. These are two separate things. However, having gone through this chapter, you should be able to find a good agent to satisfy both demands.

AGENT'S QUIZ

	YES	NO
1. Loyalty to and from an agent is vitally important?	[ ]	[ ]
2. Always go with the experienced agent?	[ ]	[ ]
3. It doesn't matter if an agent is "inactive?"	[ ]	[ ]
4. An agent must know the local area?	[ ]	[ ]
5. A good agent won't necessarily close deals?	[ ]	[ ]
6. Honesty is always the best policy?	[ ]	[ ]
7. Your agent should be a Realtor?	[ ]	[ ]
8. Recommendations don't count. It's how you feel?	[ ]	[ ]
9. Stay away from "buyer's agents?"	[ ]	[ ]
10. If you ask an agent whom they represent, they should tell you?	[ ]	[ ]

	YES	NO
11. You will never need to pay a buyer's agent?	[ ]	[ ]
12. Never work with more than one agent at a time?	[ ]	[ ]
13. The company is more important than the agent?	[ ]	[ ]
14. Working with a broker is more important than working with a salesperson?	[ ]	[ ]
15. Always try to deal directly with FSBO sellers?	[ ]	[ ]

ANSWERS

1. Yes	6. Yes	11. No
2. Yes	7. Yes	12. No
3. No	8. No	13. No
4. Yes	9. No	14. No
5. No	10. Yes	15. No

SCORING

12–15 The agent should pay you a commission!

9–11 Read your contracts closely.

5–8 You probably need an agent's help.

0–4 Hang on to your wallet!

14

Negotiating with a Seller

One way to get a more affordable property is to simply pay less. This can be accomplished by negotiating the price down with the seller. If you like to bargain, this will be your cup of tea. On the other hand, if bargaining makes you grit your teeth, then just grin and bear it. And hope for the best!

Whether or not you are successful in getting a more affordable price will depend to a large extent on how good a negotiator you are. Do a good job here and you can get a house for well under the asking price. Slip up and you'll pay more.

Let's take a look at how to do a good job of negotiating with the seller.

Working with the Purchase Agreement?

This is the tool by which negotiations are carried out. It is a document, typically four to eight pages long, written largely in legalese. It's what you fill in on the few empty spaces and in the boxes that make all the difference.

TIP

In order to be enforceable in most states, a real estate contract must be in writing. Thus, it really doesn't matter all that much what you and the seller discuss verbally. It's what you put down on paper that counts.

In filling out the purchase agreement (also sometimes called the "deposit receipt" or the "sales agreement"), you will tell the seller how much you're willing to pay and on what terms.

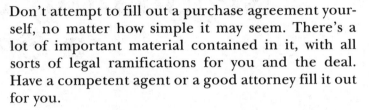

TRAP

Don't attempt to fill out a purchase agreement yourself, no matter how simple it may seem. There's a lot of important material contained in it, with all sorts of legal ramifications for you and the deal. Have a competent agent or a good attorney fill it out for you.

How Much Time Should You Give the Seller to Accept Your Offer?

We've talked about this earlier, but it bears repeating. Time is of the essence in every negotiating session. If there is no time limit, almost nothing ever gets done.

If you doubt this, think of the various telethons that are held on television or by public radio stations. If you take a close look, you'll discover that typically most of the money is raised in the last few minutes.

The telethon may be on for 40 hours. However, by hour 39 only 10 percent of the ultimate money is raised. Ninety percent comes in during that last hour.

Why? Because suddenly there's a deadline. Those who would contribute realize that either they have to act or they'll be left out.

The same thing happens with negotiations over a house. Unless there's a deadline, the sellers don't have to act. They can keep saying to themselves, the agent, and you, "We'll think it over."

You don't want the sellers thinking it over. You want them to act. They either accept, reject, or counter your offer. Action is the way to close deals. For this reason, I always suggest giving the sellers *no more* than 24 hours to accept an offer. Giving them even less is often a better idea.

TRAP

There's another problem with waiting. Another buyer may come in and slip a better offer in under yours. Agents are required to present offers as they are submitted. In other words, the sellers don't accept or reject one offer before the next one comes in. They get all offers as soon as they arrive. If they're considering yours and a better one comes in, what do you think they'll do?

How Much Should You Offer Below the Asking Price?

This is actually a loaded question since there is no single answer. The correct answer is, "It depends."

Some so-called real estate gurus state that you should always offer at least 5 percent less. Others will make it 15 percent. Both are correct, and not.

If you've done your homework, you've had your agent compile a CMA (Comparative Market Analysis) for you. It will show you how much similar homes have sold for over the past 6 months to a year. That helps you to establish the market price.

TIP

While homes may be similar, no two are identical. The lots may be larger or smaller, or better or worse located. The homes may be in better or worse shape. One home may have an amenity, such as a swimming pool, that another does not. When looking at a CMA, be sure to adjust the price up or down for these differences.

You should also have made an effort to determine just how motivated the seller is to get rid of the property (see Chapter 13 and Chapter 4). Highly motivated sellers are more likely to accept lower offers.

Finally, you have to determine just what your own demands are. If you're fighting to get into a neighborhood and simply can't

afford to offer more than a certain amount, then that will determine your price.

TRAP

We've mentioned that going in lowball is okay and that
you may need to do it 10 times before you get one
accepted. However, it's also important not to be
absurdly low. For example, offering 50 percent of the
asking price is likely to never get you an offer accepted.
Offering 25 percent off is similarly unlikely to get you
a deal, unless market conditions are terrible. More
realistic lowball offers are in the range of 5 to 20 percent off the selling price. However, every situation is
different.

Keep in mind that when you make a lowball offer, while you hope
it will be accepted, more likely you'll want to start negotiations at a
low level. However, the seller may simply reject your offer, in which
case you may be out of the deal (see below). It's the big risk you take.

What Terms Should Your Offer Contain?

Many times you can sweeten a lowball offer by coming up with better terms. For example, you may learn that the sellers want to stay
in the property an extra 3 months until their kid's school term is
up. So you agree to let them rent back the home from you, perhaps
at a very low rental rate. The sellers might be well disposed to give
you a better price.

Or perhaps the seller needs to be out within 2 weeks. You've been
pre-approved and you have your funds ready. Your ducks are all in
a row, so to speak; so you can move on a 2-week escrow (you can
close the deal in a short 2 weeks instead of the usual 30 to 45 days).
Again, the seller may be more disposed to give you a better price.

Or the sellers are retired and really would like to get some income
out of their property, which may be mostly paid off. So you arrange
to give them a second mortgage for 20 percent or more of the purchase price at the market interest rate (which is substantially higher

than the interest rate they'll get at the bank). This may be a better deal for you. And it's probably a much better deal for sellers looking for income, and that can be reflected in the price.

Remember, the terms are often what makes or breaks a deal. When you want to get the price down, consider giving the sellers a break on the terms.

What If the Seller Accepts Your Offer?

If the seller accepts your offer outright, which sometimes happens, you've bought yourself a home. However, don't celebrate quite yet. There's still a lot of work to be done. You have to actually get that big mortgage you were pre-approved for funded. And you have to close escrow. We'll have more to say about the process in the next chapter.

What If the Seller Rejects Your Offer?

This also sometimes happens. The seller simply says no and does not make a counteroffer. As noted earlier, it's more likely to happen when you lowball.

Often what the sellers are saying is that you've "insulted" them. Your offer was below their radar. They simply don't want to be bothered with it.

TIP

Sometimes when the sellers outright refuse your offer it's because they have another agenda. They may simply have decided not to sell at all, instead keeping the house. Or they have another, much higher, offer waiting in the wings. Ask your agent to see if he or she can find out what the real situation is.

You now have two choices. You can walk. Or you can come back with a better offer.

However, if you decide to come back with a better offer, keep in mind that you're negotiating from weakness. You're now saying, "I really want the place so badly that I'll pay even more than I first said I would."

When you come back with a better offer after the seller has rejected you, the seller is likely to think, "Terrific, I reject the buyers' offer and they come back higher. If I reject this second offer, the buyers are likely to come back again with a better offer still. I can keep rejecting until I get my full price!"

Remember, what you really hope for in a lowball offer is that the sellers will come back with a counteroffer and you can begin negotiations. The great risk is that the seller will simply say, "No!" and cut off further negotiations.

What If the Seller Counters?

This is the second best thing that can happen. (The best is for the sellers to accept your original offer!)

Now you have to decide whether you can accept their counteroffer or whether you should counter back yourself.

Counteroffers can go back and forth as many times as it takes to make, or lose, a deal.

TRAP

You cannot both accept and counter an offer at the same time and neither can the sellers. Either you accept the counter exactly as presented, or you make a change. The change represents a new counteroffer, which the seller can now either accept exactly as presented or counter. And on it goes.

Presumably, you'll be countering at a low level, close to your lowball original offer. Look closely, however, at the counters the seller is making.

If the sellers counter very close to the original asking price, then the sellers are telling you that they aren't likely to come down much. They are simply holding the negotiations open, waiting for you to get "realistic" and meet their price. The chances of these negotiations leading to a deal are slim.

On the other hand, if the sellers counter at way below their asking price and close to your original lowball offer, then the sellers are telling you they want out and will consider taking much less. They are now just trying to figure out how much more they can get out of you. They've already decided to go low. They're just arguing over the crumbs on the table.

If the sellers' counter is close enough to be acceptable to you, you may simply want to accept it and not risk losing the deal. (Remember, when you counter, you've in effect rejected the previous offer to you.)

On the other hand, if you feel like taking a risk, you too can argue over the crumbs. You may get the deal for the lowest possible price. Or, the sellers may at some point simply get disgusted and take their marbles and leave. My own feeling is that when the deal is close enough to be acceptable to me and the difference separating me from the sellers isn't great, I'll simply accept the sellers' last offer. Better to pay a little bit more and get the house and deal I want, than to quibble over pennies and lose out in the end.

How Long Should You Counter When You're Not Close?

Sometimes you can counter a great many times, yet never close the gap. There might, for example, be $35,000 separating your last offer from the sellers' last counter. You come up $500. The sellers come down $500. You've gone through two counters and are still $34,000 apart.

It's unlikely a situation like this is going to continue to a breakthrough. Rather, your next counter might be for $300 more and the sellers' for $200 less. In short, you're simply getting to the point of diminishing returns. You're not willing to pay what the sellers want. And they're not willing to sell for what you're willing to pay.

When Should You Send the Ultimatum?

When this happens, it may simply be time for the ultimatum. When the sellers come back with a piddling counter of, perhaps, $500 less, you might simply reject it. Send your agent back with your last counter saying it's your final, best offer. Either accept it or there's no deal.

Sometimes sellers just assume that this countering is going to continue on and on until they get what they want. Making a take-it-or-leave-it offer can bring them back to reality. Suddenly they are faced with losing out on a deal.

Of course, they may simply say, "Okay, we'll walk. There are other buyers out there."

On the other hand, they may fear losing the deal and may either accept your last offer outright or make a big drop in price in a new counter. Then negotiations can get back on track.

The ultimatum works well sometimes, but other times it results in losing the deal. I suggest never using it unless you're convinced that you already have nothing to lose—that the deal is already down the tubes.

Seller negotiations can be a lot of fun if bargaining is your fancy. But even if it's not, and it seems arduous, don't let it get you down. Always remember that it's business, not personal.

For more information, check into my book *Tips & Traps When Negotiating Real Estate* (McGraw-Hill, 1999).

SELLER'S NEGOTIATION QUIZ

	YES	NO
1. Negotiations are handled through the purchase agreement?	[ ]	[ ]
2. Time is seldom an issue?	[ ]	[ ]
3. Always low-ball by at least 15 percent?	[ ]	[ ]
4. Sweetening the terms can get you a lower price?	[ ]	[ ]
5. You can't accept an offer and counter it?	[ ]	[ ]
6. A seller can always counter your offer?	[ ]	[ ]
7. Countering can go back and forth just three times?	[ ]	[ ]
8. Sending an ultimatum will sometimes get negotiations back on track?	[ ]	[ ]

	YES	NO
9. When you low-ball, expect to only get 1 out of 10 offers accepted.	[ ]	[ ]
10. Always let the seller have 3 days to think on your offer?	[ ]	[ ]

ANSWERS

1. Yes	6. Yes
2. No	7. No
3. No	8. Yes
4. Yes	9. Yes
5. Yes	10. No

SCORING

8–10 You'll be getting your home soon.

5–7 Get your agent to help negotiate.

3–4 Get your clergyman to help negotiate.

0–2 Don't count on getting a steal anytime soon.

15

12 Steps to Buying an Affordable Home

Throughout this book, we've talked about how to get a home that's more affordable. For those who are new to the whole process, it may seem like a lot of bits and pieces. Therefore, either before you begin, or even if you're in the midst of it, getting an overview can be extremely helpful.

Here are the steps to buying a home.

Step One: Get Pre-Approved

You won't get anywhere in the buying process until you know just how much you can afford and until you can demonstrate to a seller that you'll be able to get a mortgage. The way you do this is to get yourself pre-approved by a lender.

Typically, you fill out an application and the lender will run a credit check and, perhaps, pass you by underwriting. Out of all this will come a letter usually saying how big a monthly payment you can handle. From that, you can quickly determine the size of mortgage you can afford and, thus, the most you can pay. The letter can also be shown to a seller to demonstrate your qualifications.

Now is the time to determine what kind of financing suits your needs. See Chapters 2 and 10.

Step Two: Find an Agent

Of course you can go around looking for property on your own. But why reinvent the wheel? There are already nearly a million real estate agents out there just waiting to show you properties. Find a good agent and you're halfway home in your search for an affordable home.

Review Chapter 13 for more information on getting just the right agent for you.

Step Three: Find the Property

This is the tricky part. During any given year, there are probably 7 million or more homes for sale in the United States. But you want only one, the right one.

An agent will help you see what's available in your area, but you must know what will fill your needs. Do you want three bedrooms or four? Do you want a two-story or just one? Do you want old or new?

More important, what will you be able to afford in a home? These are questions you must ask as part of your search. See Chapter 3 for more information on pricing.

Step Four: Make an Offer— Negotiate

Once you find an affordable home, there's the matter of buying it. The first step is to make an offer.

Always have your offer in writing and have it drawn up by a good real estate agent or attorney. Remember, you'll be committed to whatever you put in that offer, so make sure it's done correctly.

The sellers may either accept, reject, or counter your offer. If they counter, you're into the business of negotiation. Reread Chapter 14 for clues on how to be successful here.

Step Five: Open Escrow

"Escrow" is an independent party (usually a corporation, but you'll deal with an escrow officer). The escrow is designed to be a stake-holder who ensures that all of the wishes of both parties as expressed in the purchase agreement are fully carried out. You or your agent (or sometimes the seller) will open an escrow by placing the purchase agreement into it. Then the escrow officer will issue escrow instructions that will govern the remainder of the deal.

TRAP

The escrow instructions are designed to reflect whatever was expressed in the purchase agreement. However, sometimes escrow officers are sloppy or simply misinterpret the purchase agreement and the escrow instructions end up saying something different—something that could cost you money, time, or even the deal. Be sure to read the escrow instructions very carefully. Be sure they say exactly what was in the purchase agreement. If you're not sure, have your agent or an attorney interpret for you.

Escrow will last as long as it takes to close the deal, or until both parties agree that no deal can be closed. The purchase agreement normally will specify the time, typically 30 to 45 days. During that time you'll obtain your mortgage and the sellers will clear title to the property.

TIP

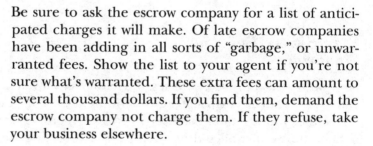

Be sure to ask the escrow company for a list of anticipated charges it will make. Of late escrow companies have been adding in all sorts of "garbage," or unwarranted fees. Show the list to your agent if you're not sure what's warranted. These extra fees can amount to several thousand dollars. If you find them, demand the escrow company not charge them. If they refuse, take your business elsewhere.

Step Six: Put Your Deposit in Escrow

An "earnest money" deposit is usually given with the purchase agreement. It signifies to the sellers that you're a serious buyer. The amount is not critical in most cases. It typically ranges from a few thousand dollars up to $10,000 or more, depending on the size of the deal. Ideally you'll put up as little as possible, yet enough to convince the sellers you're a serious buyer.

Once a purchase agreement is signed by both buyers and sellers, and escrow is opened, that deposit is typically put into escrow. It remains there until the escrow closes when it is distributed to the sellers along with other money they are to receive.

If the deal is not consummated, the deposit is either given back to you, the buyer, or kept by the sellers depending on how the purchase agreement was written and what actually happened. For example, if you have a clause in the purchase agreement saying that the sale is subject to your being able to get specific financing and you can't get it, then normally you would get your deposit back.

On the other hand, if you get your financing and then decide you'd rather not go through with the purchase and would prefer to buy another home, you might lose that money and worse, the seller might sue for damages.

The subject of deposits is very tricky and you have to be very careful on how you handle yours. You need to put it up in order to make a deal, but you also need to protect yourself so you don't lose it. For more information on deposits, ask your agent or attorney. You may also want to check into my book *Power Tips for Buying a Home for Less* (McGraw-Hill, 2000).

Step Seven: Get Your Financing

Yes, you're pre-approved. And yes, the lender says it will fund the loan. But until it actually arrives in escrow, you can't close the deal. So make sure either your agent or you keep in constant contact with the lender.

Sometimes unexpected problems arise. A credit issue could suddenly appear that requires you to track down an old creditor to have it removed. Or the lender may not approve a certain piece of paperwork that you must now redo.

TRAP

At this time, if not sooner, the lender should give you a RESPA (Real Estate Settlement Procedures Act) statement telling you what your fees will be. Ask the lender to include *all* fees, not just the RESPA ones. Then ask your agent if they are applicable. Lenders sometimes will add on unwarranted fees. Now is the time to argue over these. If the lender refuses to remove them, go to a different lender.

It's a long haul between knowing you're approved for the money and actually getting it. Sometimes the longest part of it is unexplained delays on the part of the lender who, for some strange reason, simply refuses to fund when you need the money to close. Some lenders have their own cash flow problems and are waiting for one loan to pay off before issuing another. Even a few days delay when your escrow instructions demand immediate closing could put you in jeopardy.

The rule is: call the lender at least once a week if there are no apparent problems. If there are problems, call more often. And keep on it until the problems are resolved or else you may not end up with the house!

Step Eight: Inspect the Property

It should go without saying that you would have a professional inspector check out the property as part of the purchase. This should be specified in the purchase agreement.

TIP

Most purchase agreements specify that the buyers have the right to inspect the property and that the sale is contingent on their approval of the inspection report. Typically, a time frame of two weeks or so is given for inspections. This should be extendable if something is found that requires more strenuous inspections.

Be sure to hire a professional to do this. Usually retired building inspectors do the best job. Be sure the person belongs to a national trade organization in the field such as ASHI (American Society of Home Inspectors—*www.ashi.com*) or NAHI (National Association of Home Inspectors—*www.nahi.com*).

If possible, go along with the inspector. You will be surprised at all the information you will pick up by word of mouth that isn't included in the written report.

If the property gets a clean bill of health, then you can proceed. If there are problems, you will want to negotiate with the sellers to either have them corrected or get a price reduction. If you're short of cash, a price reduction may help you enormously and then you may be able to fix the problems on your own over time.

TRAP

Lenders will want any serious problems corrected before funding your mortgage.

Step Nine: Do a Final Walk Through

Most modern purchase agreements give you the right to walk through the house just before escrow closes. The purpose is *not* to give you another opportunity to back out of the deal. It's to let you see that during the escrow period the seller has maintained the property and has not removed anything that was supposed to be included in the sale (such as a stove or chandelier).

Usually this goes fine. But if there is a problem, demand that it be corrected *before* escrow closes. If you wait until afterward, it will be much harder to get people to respond to you.

TIP

Your agent gets paid on the close of escrow. His or her motivation to get in there and resolve a tricky dispute is likely to be much lower once money is in pocket.

Usually disputes are over cleanliness and missing items. Keep in mind that when you see a home for the first time, it may have furniture in it. But when you have the final inspection, it may be empty. When the furniture is removed, spots and stains typically show up. This doesn't mean the sellers put them there recently. They may have been there all along, but hidden.

Also, sometimes fixtures that you may think go with the property actually don't. The most common example is fancy chandeliers. The sellers may take one saying it was simply screwed in. They unscrewed it, not damaging the house, and removed it. A nasty argument could ensue and there's no guarantee you'd be the winner.

If there's any personal property that's in doubt, specify that it's to be included in the sale in the purchase agreement. That way there can be no mistake.

Step Ten: Deposit Money into Escrow

Just before the deal is ready to close, you'll be asked to deposit your remaining money for the down payment and closings costs. (This is in addition to the original deposit you put up.)

Allow a couple of days for this, even if the money is in the form of a cashier's check. While you may think that a cashier's check or similar draft is as good as cash, it's not. In some unusual cases payment can be stopped. Therefore, most escrow companies want a day or so for funds to actually be transferred.

Step Eleven: Sign the Papers

These are mainly the loan papers. There may be as many as a hundred or more! You'll feel like you're signing away your life as the lender requires you to sign this and that, all toward pledging you'll pay back the mortgage.

TRAP

Some lenders will ask you to sign tax or other documents that you should not sign. Be sure you have your accountant or attorney check over your loan papers. You may want to have your attorney or accountant ask the lender to withdraw such documents. When caught in the act, lenders sometimes will.

You'll also be asked to sign final escrow instructions. These will specify where the money you are paying goes.

As you'll see, most of it goes to the sellers. Some may go for other expenses such as recording fees. Some, however, may simply be ridiculous charges on the part of the escrow company.

If you're not sure which charges are legitimate and which are unwarranted, ask your real estate agent to help you out. Most agents will know. Demand that the escrow company remove the "garbage" fees. Some will, but unfortunately some won't. At the end of the process, it's a little late to pull your only power card (the threat to take your business elsewhere).

TRAP

Recently there have been many cases reported concerning lenders throwing in unexpected fees at the very last minute. They must disclose these fees to you (called a HUD1 document) within 1 day of the closing, but by then it's often too late to do anything but protest. Often your best protection is to use a lender (mortgage broker) who comes with a recommendation from someone you know who has worked with the lender and been satisfied.

Step Twelve: Get the Key!

The house is yours. You're ready to move in. Enjoy!

TIP

As a safety precaution, be sure to get the locks changed. You wouldn't want the previous owners coming back and walking through looking for something they'd left behind!

STEPS TO CLOSING QUIZ

	YES	NO
1. Getting pre-approved is always the first step?	[ ]	[ ]
2. An agent can help you get the right deal?	[ ]	[ ]
3. Finding the right property should be first?	[ ]	[ ]
4. Negotiations are seldom necessary when purchasing?	[ ]	[ ]
5. Escrow is another name for a stakeholder?	[ ]	[ ]
6. Your deposit usually is placed in escrow?	[ ]	[ ]
7. You should start getting your loan funded as soon as escrow opens?	[ ]	[ ]
8. Using a professional inspector is a good idea?	[ ]	[ ]
9. The final walk through is your last chance to decide whether or not you want the property?	[ ]	[ ]
10. You won't need to put money for closing costs into escrow?	[ ]	[ ]
11. Paper signing is a formality?	[ ]	[ ]
12. You'll know the house is yours when you get the key?	[ ]	[ ]

ANSWERS

1. Yes	6. Yes	11. No
2. Yes	7. Yes	12. Yes
3. No	8. Yes	
4. No	9. No	
5. Yes	10. No	

SCORING

10–12 You're on your way to a new home!

7–9 It may take you a little longer.

4–6 Try re-reading the chapter.

0–3 There's always renting!

Appendix A

Amortization Table

Use the table on the following page to determine the monthly mortgage payment (principal and interest) when you already know the loan amount. Just multiply the loan amount by the factor, and you'll be given the monthly payment.

For example, say you are getting a $200,000 mortgage for 30 years at 7.25 percent interest. What are monthly payments? Simply go across to 30 years and down to 7.25. This yields the number .006822. Multiply this number times $200,000 and you discover your payment is $1,364 per month.

	Years					
Interest	3	5	7	10	15	30
7.00	.030877	.019801	.015092	.011610	.008988	.006653
7.25	.030991	.019919	.015215	.011740	.009129	.006822
7.50	.031106	.020037	.015338	.011870	.009270	.006992
7.75	.031221	.020157	.015462	.012001	.009413	.007164
8.00	.031336	.020276	.015586	.012133	.009557	.007338
8.25	.031341	.020396	.015711	.012265	.009701	.007513
8.50	.031567	.020516	.015836	.012399	.009847	.007689
8.75	.041683	.020637	.015962	.012533	.009995	.007867
9.00	.031799	.020758	.016089	.012668	.010143	.008046
9.25	.031916	.020879	.016216	.012802	.010292	.008227
9.50	.032032	.021001	.016344	.012940	.010442	.008409
9.75	.032149	.021124	.016472	.013077	.010594	.008592
10.00	.032267	.021247	.016601	.013215	.010746	.008776
10.25	.032385	.021370	.016730	.013354	.010896	.008961
10.50	.032502	.021494	.016861	.013494	.011054	.009147
10.75	.032621	.021618	.016991	.013634	.011210	.009335
11.00	.032739	.021742	.017122	.013775	.011366	.009523
11.25	.032857	.021867	.017254	.013917	.011523	.009713
11.50	.032967	.021993	.017387	.014060	.011682	.009903
11.75	.033095	.022118	.017520	.014203	.011841	.010094
12.00	.033214	.022244	.017653	.014347	.012002	.010286
12.25	.033334	.022371	.017787	.014492	.012163	.010479
12.50	.033454	.022498	.017921	.014638	.012325	.010673
12.75	.033574	.022625	.018056	.014784	.012488	.010867
13.00	.033694	.022753	.018192	.014931	.012652	.011062
13.25	.033815	.022881	.018328	.015079	.012817	.011258
13.50	.033935	.023010	.018465	.015227	.012983	.011454
13.75	.034056	.023139	.018602	.015377	.013150	.011651
14.00	.034178	.023268	.018740	.015527	.013317	.011849

Appendix B

Affordable Loan Programs

The following information comes from Freddie Mac and Fannie Mae. It refers to various loan programs. Note that while all of these are similar, they have many important differences.

Freddie Mac and Fannie Mae change their mortgage plans frequently; hence, they should not be considered written in stone. Also, although they both have plans for one- to four-family and larger units, the material here is just for single-family homes that you intend to occupy. Check with your mortgage broker or direct lender for more information.

For more information on the mortgages listed below, as well as background on Fannie Mae and Freddie Mac, check into:

www.fanniemae.com

www.freddiemac.com

Remember, neither Freddie Mac nor Fannie Mae make direct loans. They are secondary lenders. They only underwrite loans. To get one of these, you must contact a mortgage broker, bank, mortgage banker, or other direct lender.

95 Percent Mortgages from Freddie Mac

Affordable Gold 5® is a mortgage plan designed for moderate- to low-income borrowers. It only requires a 5 percent down payment (95 percent LTV) and that is quite flexible (see below). It is available on a mortgage with terms of 15, 20, and 30 years. The maximum LTV (loan to value) is 95 percent.

Down Payment.   The down payment requirement is 5 percent, plus closing costs. However, under this financing any acceptable source of nonaffordable mortgage products may be used. This typically can include cash from relatives, gifts, and other sources.

In addition, "affordable seconds" (a special Freddie Mac loan approval program for seconds) are also acceptable. In this case, the TLTV (Total Loan To Value) can be as high as 105 percent. In other words, if you don't have the cash to come up with the down payment and the closing costs, you can arrange a second mortgage to cover all of it.

Closing Costs.   These include:

Prepaids

Escrows

Financing charges

Reserves.   Most mortgage plans require that you maintain a cash reserve in the event you run into difficulty making your payments. In this case, the program "recommends" a reserve of 1 month, but does *not* require it.

Credit Qualifying.   Freddie Mac does not disclose the minimum FICO score or its own scoring policy. However, it does indicate that your monthly debt-to-income ratio should not exceed 40 percent. This simply means that you should not be paying out more than 40 percent of your income in bills each month.

Interestingly, there is no maximum housing expense-to-income ratio required. In other words, under this plan it doesn't really matter how much of your income you will need to expend on a house. Rather, each case is judged on its own merits.

TIP

In order to qualify for this mortgage, you must enroll in a class on home buying education, which includes course work on money management. Not really a bad thing for anyone.

Your income, however, may be limited to the median income in your area. In other words, this plan is not for high-income borrowers. It is intended to benefit those with a relatively modest income. Exceptions to the income barrier are available in selected high-cost areas, including the following:

- 120 percent of median in Bergen and Passaic Counties, New Jersey; Portland, Oregon; and Seattle Metro Statistical Area (MSA)
- 125 percent in Newark, New Jersey
- 135 percent in Boston MSA
- 140 percent in California
- 165 percent in New York MSA
- 170 percent in Hawaii

No income limits are applicable in concentrated areas. Concentrated areas are those that HUD (U.S. Department of Housing and Urban Development) has indicated are either a central city or a census tract in which minorities predominate.

To find more information on targeted census tracts, check into *www.freddiemac.com/sell/affgold/index.html.*

97 Percent Mortgages from Freddie Mac

This mortgage ups the ante by allowing you to come in with as little as a 3 percent down payment (97 percent LTV). In addition, you can get the money for closing costs from a variety of sources.

It is designed for low- to moderate-income families and as a result is limited to those whose incomes do not exceed the median for their areas. Exceptions are the same as for the 95 percent mortgage noted above.

Borrower Credit
- There is no maximum housing expense-to-income ratio.
- Your ratio of debt-to-income cannot be more than 40 percent.
- You must take a home buyer education program.
- You are limited in the income you can have (see above.)

Loan Type

- 97 percent LTV available on 15-, 20-, and 30-year fixed-rate mortgages. (The minimum LTV is 95.01 percent.)
- Affordable seconds are allowed to help you get the money for closing costs. However, the 3 percent down *must* be met with your own funds.

Alternate 97 Percent Mortgages from Freddie Mac

ALT 97 Mortgage.   The ALT 97® mortgage is similar to the plan noted above, except that there are no income or geographic limits.

It is designed for borrowers who have a strong credit profile, but just don't have a lot of cash to be used for the down payment and closing costs. However, you may have access to nontraditional funds such as grants, loans from a relative or even employers, or outright gifts.

This mortgage is available for 15-, 20- and 30-year fixed-rate mortgages.

Affordable Gold Alt 97.   The *Affordable Gold Alt 97*SM allows for a 97 percent mortgage, however, the down payment does not have to come from your funds. It can come from an affordable second or other sources. The alternate funds can also be used to cover the closing costs.

You do, however, have to have exemplary credit. This includes:

- A high FICO score
- At least 1 month of reserves

You also must meet income and geographic requirements. (See the 95 percent Affordable Gold mortgage above.)

This mortgage is available for 15-, 20- and 30-year fixed-rate mortgages.

Mortgages for Credit-Challenged Borrowers from Freddie Mac

The Affordable Merit Rate® mortgage is for borrowers who have had some small credit problems and, because of it, are not considered "A" borrowers, but are instead considered "A–." (See Chapter 9 for definitions of "A" and "A–.")

A– borrowers can qualify for a mortgage, but at a higher interest rate. This loan is designed to help those borrowers get more affordable financing.

What makes this loan most interesting is that it not only offers a lower initial interest rate for a credit-challenged borrower, but if the borrower is able to make 24 consecutive on-time mortgage payments within a 4-year qualifying period, the interest rate is reduced by 1 percent. (Quite an incentive!)

Freddie Mac says not only does this loan offer reduced rates, but it also helps a borrower who might be having troubles to establish a record of good credit management.

Borrower Credit

- The borrower may be A–, which means that he or she was delinquent in a loan payment as many as two times over the previous years.

- The borrower can't have 30-day or more delinquencies more than twice in the prior 12 months.

- The borrower may have limited funds available for a down payment, hence the relatively high LTV ratios.

- The borrower may incur lots of debt, provided there is a logical explanation such as divorce, medical payments, or job loss.

- The borrower must be able to pay up on any late or unpaid debt, bringing it current.

- The monthly ratio of the borrower's debt payment to income can't be greater than 50 percent.

- The borrower can't have bankruptcies within the past 24 months and no foreclosure in the previous 36 months.

Loan Type. Freddie Mac offers this type of underwriting on a standard fixed-rate loan (15, 20, or 30 years) as well as mortgages with a balloon payment after 7 years (converting to an ARM). The loan is also available as an ARM. Affordable second financing may also be available in some cases.

The LTV may be as high as 90 percent for 30-year loans. However, in that case, 30 percent mortgage insurance is required. For 15- or

20-year loans, the LTV is a maximum of 90 percent with 25 percent mortgage insurance.

TRAP

Any mortgage with an LTV of over 80 percent requires private mortgage insurance. This insures the lender, but not the borrower, against loss. It insures the lender for the "top" of the mortgage— the first money lost—anywhere from the top 5 to 40 percent. The greater the percent, the higher the premium. You, the borrower, get stuck with the premium, which can be as much as half a percent or more of the mortgage annually. Mortgage insurance is a necessary evil. It costs us more money. But it allows us to get higher LTVs.

100 Percent Mortgage from Freddie Mac

This is a special plan for borrowers who don't have the cash for a down payment, or who have the cash but don't want to use it. It offers them a 100 percent LTV. It's a true "nothing down" plan.

In addition, funds for purchasing the home may come from a gift from a related person.

Credit Requirements

- You must have excellent credit, meaning that you should be an "A" borrower (see definitions in Chapter 9).

- You can have had no bankruptcy, foreclosures, or have given a deed in lieu of foreclosure during the 7 years prior to applying for this loan.

- Your maximum debt-to-income ratio can be 41 percent.

- No income limits (you don't have to be below a certain income level), except in the case of affordable second mortgages.

TRAP

When faced with foreclosure, some savvy borrowers will instead get the lenders to accept a deed back to them in lieu of going through with the foreclosure. This saves the lender time and money. It saves the borrower having a foreclosure on his or her records. However, this became so rampant during the 1990s that today having a "deed in lieu" on your record is tantamount to having a foreclosure. Some lenders today simply won't accept the deed in lieu, but will instead proceed through foreclosure.

The Loan.   This is one of those mortgages that we tend to fantasize about. For those with limited funds and good credit, it's a dream. It allows:

- 100 percent LTV (up to 103 percent with affordable seconds for those who have limited incomes). The mortgage insurance must be 40 percent.
- Only 3 percent borrower funds, to be used for either the down payment or closing costs. The 3 percent can even be in the form of sweat equity!

TIP

Sweat equity simply means that you contribute your time and labor toward fixing up the property. It counts in lieu of cash toward the down payment, closing costs, or both.

- The seller of the property can contribute up to 3 percent of the mortgage amount toward the borrower's closing costs and prepaid expenses.
- A related person can contribute up to 3 percent of the mortgage amount. (When gifts are made, there is usually 5 percent down payment required from other sources. This is waived for this loan.)

The Property.   As with all mortgages, the property must appraise for the sales price to receive the higher mortgage value. However, the appraisal must indicate that the property is *not* located in an area where real estate market values are declining.

Second Mortgages at Freddie Mac

Freddie Mac now approves second mortgages. These can then be used to supplement your down payment or closing costs. They allow you to help qualify for a fixed-rate mortgage otherwise available through Freddie Mac.

This increases your flexibility when you're cash poor and are having trouble coming up with the down payment, but are otherwise a good credit risk. These are generally available to low- and moderate-income borrowers.

(*Note:* While Freddie Mac purchases first mortgages, it does not purchase the second mortgage. That has to be arranged between yourself and your lender.)

Fixed-Rate Mortgage from Fannie Mae

Just like Freddie Mac, Fannie Mae also has a large variety of mortgages available for those who have affordability issues. Below is a summary of some of its more popular fixed-rate products.

Pledged Asset Mortgages.   Pledged Asset mortgages offer up to 100 percent LTV financing. They are available to borrowers who show a large enough income to handle the mortgage and who have good credit, but are short on cash. Fannie Mae's flagship here is its Flexible 100® mortgage plan.

Fannie 97 and Flexible 97 Mortgages.   Fannie 97® offers a 97 percent LTV mortgage. The 3 percent cash down, however, must come from the borrower's funds. However, the reserve requirement is only for 1 month's worth of mortgage payments.

There are, however, income and geographic area restrictions. And the borrower must participate in face-to-face education programs.

The loan can be from 15 to 30 years. Up to 38 percent of the borrower's monthly income can be used for housing costs and other debts, such as credit cards or student loans. Fully a third of the borrower's income can be aimed entirely at housing costs. Another similar mortgage, Flexible 97® offers lower-cost mortgage insurance.

Timely Payment Rewards Mortgage.   Timely Payment Rewards® is a mortgage designed to help borrowers who have less than "A" creditworthiness. If the borrower goes 2 years without a 30-day delinquency within the first 4 years of the loan, he or she will receive an interest-rate reduction. (It's handled automatically, so you don't have to write in for your reward!)

Interest First Mortgage Plan. Interest First® is an unusual mortgage plan designed to help affordability by giving you the lowest possible mortgage payment. The way it works is unique.

Under Interest First, your mortgage payment is based entirely on interest for the first 15 years. Starting at year 16, your payment includes principal with the mortgage amortizing (fully paying off) within the remaining 15 years. Thus, the first half of the loan you pay interest only. The second half you pay interest and principal.

While this may seem like a terrific solution, it's important to note that in the initial years of a mortgage the amount that goes to principal is not high. For example, in a $100,000 30-year mortgage at 7 percent interest, the portion of the monthly payment that goes to principal in the first month is only about $80. Thus, if the principal portion is eliminated, the monthly payment is reduced by only a few dollars.

On the other hand, if at year 16 you begin making payments on both principal and interest, the mortgage payment could suddenly jump by as much as 20 percent because you've only got 15 years to pay back the principal.

TIP

A savvy borrower would only keep this loan until year 15, then refinance or sell the property. The downside is that you're not contributing anything to your equity— you're not paying off the mortgage. At the end of 15 years, you would owe as much as you did when you first obtained the financing.

Adjustable-Rate Mortgages from Fannie Mae

Fannie Mae also offers a large array of ARMs. These offer 3-, 5-, 7-, and 10-year fixed-interest rate periods. After the initial fixed-rate period, the mortgage converts to an adjustable.

LIBOR indexed mortgages offer a 6-month teaser. The LIBOR index is suggested as inhibiting wide swings in interest rates that could adversely affect the borrower. (Indeed, the LIBOR has historically been a stable barometer of the interest-rate market. See Chapter 10.)

Two-Step® is a mortgage with only one adjustment. Fannie Mae's ARM 975 adjusts after 7 years. Its ARM 1029 adjusts after 5 years. In both cases, the new interest rate is determined based on the weekly average of 10-year Treasury securities (adjusted to a constant maturity) plus a margin.

TIP

The 10-year Treasury securities index has been widely used for adjusting fixed-rate mortgages ever since the demise of the 30-year Treasury bond.

Fannie Mae also offers another unusual and potentially beneficial product, its 7-year balloon mortgage.

Here, the monthly payments are based on a 30-year mortgage. However, the interest rate is based on a lower-rate 7-year mortgage. At year 7, the mortgage converts to a 23-year, fixed-rate mortgage based on market interest rates. Of course, the conversion assumes the borrower has maintained the mortgage in good standing during the first 7 years.

Index

Adjustable-rate mortgage (ARM), 8
  basics of, 134
  "catch-up" clauses for, 140
  common elements of, 134
  consumer strategy for, 133
  convertible option of, 147–148
  from Fannie Mae, 219–220
  fixed-rate mortgage vs., 132
  index and, 134–137
  indices for, 135–136
  interest-rate caps and, 141
  from lender's perspective, 133–134
  monthly payment and, 131–132
  mortgage payment caps and, 141–142
  steps and, 139–140
  teaser rate and, 132–133
  types of, 146–147
Adjustment period for adjustable-rate
    mortgage, 138
Adviser(s):
  contractor-carpenter as, 100
  hiring agent as, 182–183
  hiring architect as, 97–98
  for lender's expert requirement, 93
Affordability:
  high prices and, 23–27
  smallest lot, worst house and, 26
Affordable Gold Alt 97, 155
Affordable Gold 5, 152, 155
  closing costs and, 212
  credit qualifying for, 212
  details of, 212–213
  down payment and, 212
  exceptions for, 213
  reserves and, 212
Affordable Gold 97, 153, 155
Affordable Gold 3/2, 155
Affordable Merit Rate, 153
  borrower credit and, 215
  from Freddie Mac, 215–216
  loan types offered, 215–216

Affordable Seconds, 155
Agent(s):
  "active" status of, 175
  buyers, affordability issues and, 171
  buying a home and, 199–200
  closing of deal by, 176–177
  dual, 190
  experience of, 175
  fixer-uppers and, 74, 83
  honesty of, 177–178
  independent vs. national company,
      185–186
  interviewing of, 175
  knowledge of area by, 176
  lowball offers and, 173–174
  loyal buyer and, 172
  loyalty of, 171–173
  recommendations for, 178
  representation of, 179–180
  trade organizations and, 178
  "vest pocket listing" and, 184
  working with, 183–184
Alt 97 Mortgage from Freddie Mac, 214
Alternative financing, 7–8
American Society of Home Inspectors
    (ASHI), 203
Amortization table, monthly mortgage
    payment and, 209–210
Appliances and fixtures, installation of,
    106
Approved property, FHA loan and,
    162–163
Architect, set fee arrangement for, 98
ARM (see Adjustable-rate mortgage)
Assets for home purchase, 17–20
Average cost of mortgage rate, 136

Biannual (mortgage):
  mortgage adjustment period as, 139
  second mortgage and, 139
Board of Directors, 42, 48

221

Borrower, rating of, 113, 114
Broker:
  drawbacks of, 186
  with national company, 186
  working with salesperson vs.,
    184–185
Budgeting, 17
Building process:
  final financing and, 106–107
  "finaled" by building department,
    106
  financing lot for, 94–95
  finding, buying lot for, 94
  finishing of, 105–106
  installation of electrical, plumbing,
    heating for, 103
Buy, Rent, and Sell (Irwin), 35
Buyer's agent, 178–179
  advantages of, 180–181
  agreement with, 182, 183
  "cobroking" deal with, 182
  commission for, 181–182
  commitment, loyalty of, 183
  negotiation of commission with, 182
  up-front fees for, 182–183

Carpentry, finishing of, 105–106
Carry back:
  with fixer-upper, 85
  and home construction, 94
Cash reserves for mortgage loan, 118
CC&Rs (*see* Covenants, Conditions, and
    Restrictions)
Certificate of Reasonable Value (CRV),
    166–167
championhomes.com, 52
Closing costs, 10, 59, 86
Closing expenses, 3
  (*See also* Closing costs)
Co-operative(s), 39
  as alternative to homes, 50
  concerns of, 46–50
  condominiums vs., 41
  considerations for buying, 43–46
  cost of home vs., 40–42
  fees for, 48
  good deals on, 43–46

Co-operative(s) (*Cont.*):
  insurance for, 48
  lawsuits and, 47
  layout of, 45
  lifestyle of homes vs., 39–40
  lighting and, 45
  location features of, 44–46
  noise and, 44
  rental ratio and, 46–47
  reserves in, 47–48
  rules of, 49–50
  safety of, 45
  size of, 45–46
  view in, 44
Community Land Trust, 159
Community Seconds, 159
Comparative Market Analysis (CMA),
    191
Condition, mobile homes and, 52–53
Condominium(s), 39
  as alternative to homes, 50
  co-operatives vs., 41
  concerns of, 46–50
  considerations for buying, 43–46
  cost of home vs., 40–42
  fees for, 48
  good deals on, 43–46
  insurance and, 48
  lawsuits and, 47
  layout of, 45
  lifestyle of homes vs., 39–40
  lighting and, 45
  location features of, 44–46
  noise in, 44
  rental ratio and, 46–47
  reserves in, 47–48
  rules of, 49–50
  safety in, 45
  size of, 45–46
  view in, 44
Conforming loan, 151
Construction loan, 91–92, 94, 106
Contractor:
  construction loan and, 93
  hiring of, 99–100
Contractor-carpenter, 93
Conversions, 41

Convertible mortgage:
  advantages of, 147–148
  conversion fee for, 148
Cosigner:
  agreements for, 129
  necessity of, 128–129
Cosmetic problems, 28
Cost of home ownership, 3–4
Cost of Funds index, 136
Counteroffer, 194
  large gap between, 195
  ultimatum to, 195–196
Covenants, Conditions, and
  Restrictions (CC&Rs), 28
"Creative financing," 11
Credit, 10–11
  correction of error on, 125
  credit bureau mistakes and, 124–125
  establishing of, 126–127
  explanations for lender and,
    123–124
  fixing of, 120–122
  importance of, 109–110, 129
  interest rate and, 153
Credit bureau, corrections of errors by,
  124–125
Credit-challenged:
  Freddie Mac mortgages and, 214–216
  loan programs for, 152, 153
Credit check, 16, 111
Credit history:
  creation of, 128
  Fannie Mae, Freddie Mac loan
    programs and, 154
Credit lines, loan approval and, 119
Credit rating, improvement of, 115
Credit report:
  analysis of, 111
  evaluation of score on, 111–112
  obtaining copy of, 126
Credit requirements:
  of 95 percent Freddie Mac mortgage,
    212
  of 100 percent Freddie Mac mortgage,
    216
  of Affordable Merit Rate Freddie
    Mac mortgage, 215

Credit score, 151
cyberhomes.com, 35

Debt, loan approval and, 118–119
Density, condominiums and
    co-operatives and, 44
Deposit (see Earnest money deposit)
Deposit receipt, 189
  (See also Purchase agreement)
Developed lot, 95
Down payment, 3, 86
  Fannie Mae, Freddie Mac loan
    programs and, 154
  loan programs and, 117, 153
Drywall, tape, and texture, installation
    of, 104–105
Dual agent, advantage and
    disadvantage of, 180

Earnest money deposit:
  escrow and, 201–202
  protection of, 202
Electrical, finishing of, 105
eloan.com, 5, 17
Entitlement, VA loans and, 165
Equifax, 111
Equity, 20–21
Escrow:
  deposit into, 205
  final instructions for, 206
  opening of, 200
Escrow instructions, purchase
    agreement and, 201
Experion, 111
experion.com, 111

fairisaac.com, 111
Fannie Mae, 112
  adjustable-rate mortgages and,
    219–220
  contact information for, 168
  credit and, 154
  credit-challenged and, 152
  Fannie 97 and, 152
  Fannie 97 mortgages from, 218
  fixed-rate mortgage from, 218–219
  Flexible 97 mortgages from, 218

Fannie Mae (*Cont.*):
  mortgage programs from, 152–153,
    155, 159–160
  Pledged Asset mortgages from, 218
  as underwriter, 151
fanniemae.com, 31
Fannie Mae mortgage programs, 211,
  218–220
  income requirements for, 154
  where to find, 155
Fannie Neighbors, 159
Fannie 97, 152, 153
  from Fannie Mae, 218
Farming of neighborhoods, 25
Federal Emergency Management
  Agency (FEMA), 158
  contact information for, 168
Federal Home Loan Bank Board, 145
Federal Housing Administration
  (FHA), 158
  advantage of, 160
  limitations of, 161–162
  mortgage programs from,
    160, 161
  second mortgage programs from,
    161
Federal Housing Administration (FHA)
  mortgages:
  advantages of, 163–164
  assumability of, 163–164
  impounds and, 164
  information on, 160–161
  prepayment penalties and, 164
  qualifying rules for, 162–163
Federal Reserve Board, 136
Federal Trade Commission, 125
Fee-for-service agent, 60, 61
Fees, condominiums and co-operatives
  and, 48–49
FICO (Fair Isaac), 111
Financial profiles:
  Fannie Mae and, 151
  Freddie Mac and, 151
Financial profiling, 14
  financing and, 112–113
Financing:
  building process and, 106–107

Financing (*Cont.*):
  credit score and, 113
  of fixer-upper, 70–72
  of home building, 90, 91
  interest rate and, 7
  mobile homes and, 53
  securing of, 202
First-time home buyer:
  definition of, 157–158
  programs for, 157, 158
"Fixed/adjustable" mortgage,
  146–147
Fixed-rate mortgage:
  adjustable-rate mortgage vs., 8, 132
Fixer-upper, 69
  agents and, 74
  costs of, 78–79
  description of, 69–70
  evaluation of, 77–79, 80–81
  expired listings and, 76
  financial commitment of, 70
  financing of, 70–72
  finding of, 73–77
  first-time, 80
  flyers and, 77
  FSBO as, 77
  funds needed for, 86–87
  inspection and, 85
  MLS and, 74
  newspapers, Internet postings and,
    77
  offer price for, 81–82
  overestimation of skills for, 82
  presentation of offer for, 83–85
  reasons for, 73
  serious problems of, 79–80
  structuring deal for, 85–86
  timing of funds for, 72–73
  traps of, 85
"Flag" lot, 26, 27
fleetwood.com, 52
Flexible 97 mortgage from Fannie
  Mae, 218
For Sale By Owner (FSBO), 25
  agreement for, 63
  benefits of, 57–58
  closing costs and, 59

For Sale By Owner (FSBO) (*Cont.*):
  definition of, 57–58
  Internet and, 35
  reduced price and, 58–59
For Sale By Owner (FSBO) deal:
  buyer's agent and, 66
  closing of, 61
  inspection, repairs and, 60–61
  paperwork for, 60
For Sale By Owner (FSBO) properties,
  as fixer-uppers, 77
For Sale By Owner (FSBO) seller:
  finding of, 64
  introduction to, 64–65
  negotiation with, 58–59, 61–63
For Sale By Owner Kit, The (Irwin), 66
Foreclosure properties, 34–35
  types of, 34–35
Foundation, inspection of, 101–102
Framing of house, 102
Freddie Mac, 112
  Affordable Gold 5 and, 152
  Affordable Gold 5 mortgage from,
    211–213
  Affordable Gold Alt 97 from, 214
  Alt 97 mortgage from, 214
  contact information for, 168
  credit and, 154
  credit-challenged and, 152
  loan incentives from, 153
  loan programs from, 152–153, 155
  97 percent mortgage from,
    213–214
  100 percent mortgage from,
    216–217
  second mortgages from, 217–218
  as underwriter, 151
Freddie Mac mortgage programs,
  211–218
  for credit-challenged borrowers,
    214–216
  income requirements for, 154
  where to find, 155
FSBO (*see* For Sale By Owner)

Ginnie Mae, 151
Grading of lot, 100

Handyman specials (*see* Fixer-upper)
Heating, finishing of, 105
Highly motivated seller, 32–34
  reasons for, 33
HOA (*see* Home Owners Association)
Home, building of, 89
Home construction:
  cost savings of, 91
  difficulty of, 89
  experts, financing and, 93
  financing of, 91
  steps in, 90
Home Depot, 106
Home Owners Association (HOA), 40,
  42, 48
  rules, restrictions of, 49–50
Home ownership:
  down payment and, 3
  mortgage payment and, 3
Home purchase, steps to, 199–206
homepath.com, 160
Hookup (*see* Sewer hookup)
HUD (*see* U.S. Department of Housing
  and Urban Development)
Hybrid mortgage, 138–139

Impounds, Veterans Affairs (VA)
    mortgage programs and, 167
Income:
  Fannie Mae, Freddie Mac loan
    programs and, 154
  loan qualification and, 116–117
Index:
  adjustable-rate mortgage and, 134–137
  selection of lender and, 137
Indices, 135–136
Inspection:
  financing and, 106
  of fixer-upper, 85
  FSBO deal and, 60–61
  as step to buying home, 203–204
Insulation, installation of, 104
Insurance:
  condominiums and co-operatives
    and, 48
  determining costs of, 5
Interest, 4, 5, 49

Interest First mortgage, 155,
   219
Interest rate, 4
   calculation of, 4–5
   credit requirements and, 153
   paycheck and, 7
   steps and, 139–140
   (*See also* Subprime)

Interest-rate cap:
   on adjustable-rate mortgage, 141
   monthly payment cap and, 146
Internet, home listings on, 35, 77

"Key" lot, 26, 27

Labor, 87
Lawsuits, condominiums and
   co-operatives and, 47
Layout, condominiums and
   co-operatives and, 45
Lease option, 157
Lease Purchase, 159–160
Lenders:
   acceptable explanations for,
      123–124
   adjustable-rate mortgage benefits to,
      133–134
   borrower ratings of, 114
   cosigners on loan and, 128–129
   fees and, 202–203
   home construction and, 91–93
   rating system of, 113
lendingtree.com, 17
LIBOR (London Interbank Offered
   Rate) index, 136–137
Loan, takeout, 91, 92, 94, 106
Loan application, standard, 110
Loan papers, signing of, 205
Loan to value (LTV), 15
   financing and, 113
   on fixer-upper, 70–71
   "takeout" loan and, 92
Location, 23–25
   condominiums and co-operatives
      and, 43–46
   (*See also* Neighborhood)

London Interbank Offered Rate
   (LIBOR), 136–137
Lot:
   building plans for, 97–98
   drainage and, 95
   financing for, 94
   finding, buying, 94
   foundation for, 101
   grading of, 100
   pitfalls of, 95–96
   plans for, 98–99
   roads and, 95–96
   sewer hookup on, 96–97
   site of, 96
   soil on, 96
   survey of, 96
   things to look for in, 95–96
   trees on, 96
   utilities and, 95
Low-cash down financing, 10
Low-interest, low-down financing, 31
Lowball offer, 29, 32, 174
   considerations for, 191–192
   counteroffer to, 194–195
   rejection of, 193–194
   terms of, 192–193
LTV (*see* Loan to value)
Lycos, 35

Margin, 137–138
Materials, 87
Mechanic's liens, 71, 107
MLS (*see* Multiple Listing Service)
Mobile homes, 39, 50–54
   benefits of, 50–51
   condition of, 52–53
   definition of, 51
   financing for, 53
   finding information on, 52
   negotiability of, 53
   pitfalls of, 52–53
   rental rates for, 53
Monthly payment, 3, 131
   adjustable-rate mortgage and,
      131–132
   taxes and, 5–6
   (*See also* Mortgage payment)

Monthly payment cap, interest-rate cap and, 146
Mortgage broker, loan pre-approval and, 16
Mortgage Credit Certificate (MCC), 158
Mortgage insurance, LTV and, 215–216
Mortgage insurance premium, FHA loan and, 163
Mortgage interest, 5–6
Mortgage loan:
  applications for, 110–111
  cash reserves and, 118
  conditional approval on, 120
  cosigners on, 128–129
  dispute with creditor and, 122
  down payment and, 117
  income and, 116–117
  income vs. expenses and, 115–116
  lack of credit and, 128
  low, no-cash down financing and, 10
  pre-approval for, 14–15
  repayment of debts and, 118
  self-employment and, 116
  size of income and, 116–117
Mortgage payment:
  affordability of, 13–15
  amortization table and, 209–210
  budgeting for, 18
  calculation of, 18
  caps on, 141–142
  points and, 9
Mortgage payment cap:
  adjustable-rate mortgage and, 141–142
  rate comparison of, 145
  steps and, 142
  trade-offs for, 144
Mortgage programs, finding information on, 158–159
mortgage.com, 5
Multiple Listing Service (MLS), 29, 178
  expired listings on, 76
  fixer-uppers listed on, 74

National Association of Home Inspectors (NAHI), 203

National Association of Realtors, 178, 185
Negative amortization, 142–143
  avoidance of, 144
  payment caps and, 142–144
Negotiating:
  of mobile homes, 53
  with seller, 189
  as step to buying a home, 200
Neighborhood:
  access and, 25
  crime rate and, 24
  criteria for, 24–25
  development and, 24–25
  farming of, 25
  pride and, 24
  schools and, 24
97 percent mortgage:
  borrower credit and, 213
  loan type of, 214
No-cash down financing, 10
Noise, condominiums and co-operatives and, 44
"Nonrecurring" closing costs, 59

Offer:
  acceptance of, 193
  asking price and, 191
  rejection of, 193–194
  as step to buying home, 200
100 percent mortgage, 153
  credit requirement and, 216
  from Freddie Mac, 216–217
  loan details of, 217
Open house, 179
Owner-occupied, FHA loan and, 162

P and I (*see* Principal; Interest)
Paid evaluations, 86
Painting, 106
Paperwork, 60
Partnership sharing arrangement, 20–21
Payment (*see* Monthly payment; Mortgage payment)
PITI (principal, interest, taxes, and insurance), 4, 49, 115
  true monthly cost of, 4–5
  (*See also* Mortgage payment)

Planned Unit Developments (PUDs), 43
Pledged Asset mortgage, 155
    from Fannie Mae, 218
Plumbing, finishing of, 105
Points, 8–9
    interest rate and, 9–10
Power Tips for Buying a Home for Less
    (Irwin), 202
Pre-approval:
    credit check and, 16
    as first step to buying home, 199
    of loan, 14–15
    mortgage broker and, 16
    pre-qualified vs., 15–16
    sources for, 16–17
    trouble with, 15–16
Pre-qualified, pre-approval vs.,
    15–16
Prepayment penalties of adjustable-rate
    mortgages, 144–145
Principal, 4
    calculation of, 4–5
Profit, 87
Property, finding of, 200
Property sharing, 20–21
    (*See also* Equity)
Property tax, paycheck and, 7
Provisional approval, 151
Purchase agreement:
    deadline for, 190
    escrow instructions and, 201
    home inspection and, 203
    importance of, 189

quicken.com, 5, 17

Real Estate Owned (REO), 34, 174
Real Estate Settlement Procedures Act
    (RESPA), lender's fees and,
    202–203
Realtor, 185
realtor.com, 35
Rental rate, mobile homes and, 53
Rental ratio, condominiums and co-
    operatives and, 46–47
REO (*see* Real Estate Owned)

Repossessions, 174
Reserves, condominiums and
    co-operatives and, 47–48
Roof, installation of, 102–103
Run-down properties (*see* Fixer-upper)
Rules of condominiums and
    co-operatives, 49–50

Safety, condominiums and co-operatives
    and, 45
Sales agreement (*see* Purchase
    agreement)
Self-employment and loan
    consideration, 116
Seller:
    counteroffer from, 194
    motivation of, 33, 191
    ultimatum to, 195–196
Sewer hookup, 96–97
Single-family home:
    buying foreclosure of, 34–35
    differences from condos and co-ops,
        40
    of Internet, 35
    lowball offers on, 29–30
    neighborhood and, 23–26
    search for, 23
    similarities to condos and co-ops, 39
    smallest lot, worst house and, 26–29
    turn-around area for, 30–32
Site, for building, 96
Skin of house, 103–104
skylinecorp.com, 52
Standard factual, 111
    (*See also* Credit check)
Standard loan application, 110
Steps:
    adjustable-rate mortgage and,
        139–140
    mortgage payment caps and, 142
    teaser rate and, 140
Strict qualifying, FHA loan and, 163
Subcontractors, hiring of, 99–100
Subprime:
    borrowers as, 113–114
    finding mortgage for, 115
Sweat equity, 69–70, 82, 153, 217

Takeout loan, 91, 92, 94, 106
Taxes:
  determining costs of, 5
  monthly payments and, 5–6
  mortgage interest payments, 5–6
  tax breaks, deductions and, 5–6
Tear down, 86
Teaser rate, steps and, 140
Terms for lowball offer, 192–193
Timely Payment Rewards mortgage,
    153, 155
  from Fannie Mae, 218–219
Timing of funds for fixer-upper, 72–73
*Tips & Traps When Negotiating Real
    Estate* (Irwin), 196
*Tips & Traps When Renovating Your
    Home* (Irwin), 71, 86, 107
*Tips and Traps When Buying a Condo or
    Co-op* (Irwin), 50, 65
Title I from Federal Housing
    Administration, 161
Title II from Federal Housing
    Administration, 161
Townhouse, 42–43
Trade-off, mortgage payment cap, 144
Trailer parks, 39
  (*See also* Mobile homes)
Transaction costs, 87
Transunion, 111
Treasury bills, 8, 135
Treasury securities index, 136
Turn-around area, 30–31
  attributes of, 31–32
  bargain of, 32
  crime and, 32
  local attraction in, 31
  work in progress in, 31

Underwriter, pre-approval and, 16
Underwriting process, 16
Undeveloped lot, 95
U.S. Department of Housing and Urban
    Development (HUD), 158, 213

Veterans Affairs (VA):
  mortgage programs from, 165
  qualifications for, 165–166
Veterans Affairs (VA) mortgage
    programs, 165
  assumability of, 167
  entitlement and, 165–166, 167
  impounds and, 167
  securing of, 166
View, condominiums and co-operatives
    and, 44

Walk-through before closing escrow,
    204–205
Web sites:
  championhomes.com, 52
  cyberhomes.com, 35
  eloan.com, 5, 17
  experion.com, 111
  fairisaac.com, 111
  fanniemae.com, 31
  fleetwood.com, 52
  homepath.com, 160
  lendingtree.com, 17
  mortgage.com, 5
  quicken.com, 5, 17
  realtor.com, 35
  skylinecorp.com, 52

Yahoo, 35
Yield, 9

About the Author

Robert Irwin, one of America's leading experts in all areas of real estate, is the author of more than 50 books. His Tips and Traps series for McGraw-Hill has sold over a million copies. A broker and property investor as well as an adviser to consumers and agents, he has helped buyers and sellers solve their real estate problems for more than 20 years. He lives in Westlake Village, California. For more real estate tips and traps, go to www.robertirwin.com.